*The Journey of the Fifth Horse*

*Harry, Noon and Night*

# The
# Journey of the Fifth Horse

## AND

# Harry, Noon and Night

*two plays by*

## RONALD RIBMAN

LITTLE, BROWN AND COMPANY · BOSTON · TORONTO

We are grateful for permission to reprint the following copyrighted
material:
"The Man with the Blue Guitar" from *The Collected Poems of Wal-
lace Stevens* (1954). Reprinted by permission of Alfred A. Knopf,
Inc., publishers.
"The Fuehrer's Face" from *Donald Duck in Nutsyland* by Oliver
Wallace. Copyright 1942 by Southern Music Publishing Company
Inc. Used by permission.

*Published simultaneously in Canada*
*by Little, Brown & Company (Canada) Limited*

PRINTED IN THE UNITED STATES OF AMERICA

# The Journey of the Fifth Horse

*A two-act play based, in part, on the story
"Diary of a Superfluous Man"
by
Ivan Turgenev*

# The Original Cast

(*in order of appearance*)

TERENTIEVNA, *housekeeper to Nikolai Alexeevich Chulkaturin*
Mary Hayden

ZODITCH, *first reader in the Grubov Publishing Company*
Dustin Hoffman

SERGEY, *grandchild of Terentievna*                Christopher Strater

*RUBIN, *apprentice reader in the Grubov Publishing Company*
William H. Bassett

†MISS GRUBOV, *owner of the Grubov Publishing Company*
Susan Anspach

‡PANDALEVSKI, *supervising printer in the Grubov Publishing
    Company*                                      Lee Wallace

KATERINA PROLOMNAYA, *a landlady*          Catherine Gaffigan

NIKOLAI ALEXEEVICH CHULKATURIN, *a landowner*   Michael Tolan

DOCTOR KORVIN, *a physician*                     Mark Hammer

LEVINOV, *a lawyer*                               Harry Miller

§FEATHERS, *a cleaning girl*                     Susan Lipton

KIRILLA MATVEICH OZHOGIN, *a landowner*           Allan Rich

†ELIZAVETA KIRILLOVNA, *his daughter*          Susan Anspach

‡BIZMIONKOV, *family friend of the Ozhogins*      Lee Wallace

ANNA, *wife of Kirilla*                      Martha Greenhouse

GREGORY, *a neighbor to Zoditch*                   Jack Aaron

§VOLOBRINA, *a servant girl*                     Susan Lipton

*CAPTAIN IVAN PETROVICH NARVINSKY, *a cavalry officer*
William H. Bassett

TANIA, *an unmarried girl*                      Jane Buchanan

LIEUTENANT ZIMIN, *a cavalry officer*                                 Jim Doerr
OFFICERS                                                      Brian Turkington
                                                                   Ron Seka

### The following roles are doubled:

\*RUBIN and CAPTAIN IVAN PETROVICH NARVINSKY
†MISS GRUBOV and ELIZAVETA KIRILLOVNA
‡PANDALEVSKI and BIZMIONKOV
§FEATHERS and VOLOBRINA

The first performance of *The Journey of the Fifth Horse* was given on April 13, 1966, at the American Place Theatre in New York City. It was directed by Larry Arrick. The scenery and costumes were by Kert Lundell; the lighting by Roger Morgan.

# ACT ONE

# ACT TWO

TIME:  The late nineteenth century
PLACE:  St. Petersburg, Russia

# Act One

# Scene One

PLACE: *An office space in the Grubov Publishing House occupied by* ZODITCH *and* RUBIN.

TIME: *Late afternoon.*

SCENE: *There are two desks:* RUBIN's *on the left side of the room;* ZODITCH's *on the right side.*

ON RISE: *The stage is completely dark. We hear a voice.*

VOICE

In Samarkand I saw a monkey yellow-splotched and dying in a cage, and as I made to hasten by, he grasped my sleeve as if there might be something more to the matter.

(*Lights up*)

RUBIN, *a young man of about twenty-five years of age, sits behind his desk tweezing and clipping his moustache. His desk is bare, in rather sharp contrast to the fairly well-cluttered desk of* ZODITCH.

ZODITCH *stands on a little ladder near the back wall of the room, engaged in hanging a border of black crepe around a large portrait of* MR. GRUBOV, *the founder of the firm.*

ZODITCH *is about ten years older than* RUBIN. *He is thin, wiry, quick and nervous in his movements. When he puts*

[ 11 ]

*his glasses on you can hardly see his eyes. He is of somewhat less than average height, and losing his hair.*

*In front of* ZODITCH's *desk sit two visitors:* TERENTIEVNA, *a peasant woman in her early sixties, and her grandson* SERGEY, *about seventeen years old — a simple-minded boy who is stylishly dressed in clothes that are obviously too small for him. His arms dangle out of his sleeves. The clothes seem ready to burst.*

TERENTIEVNA
(*To* ZODITCH)
Did you say something, mister?

ZODITCH
No.

TERENTIEVNA
Oh, I thought you said something. I thought you was saying you wanted to read the writing, mister.

ZODITCH
I said nothing, madam. I am hanging the crepe now.

TERENTIEVNA
Because if you want I can let you read the writing now, mister.

ZODITCH
(*Exasperated*)
I cannot read your master's manuscript now, madam. I am hanging the crepe now. You have come at a bad time. There has been a death in the firm; our employer, Mr. Grubov, has passed away.

TERENTIEVNA

Oh, has he?

ZODITCH

Yes.

TERENTIEVNA

That's a sorrow.

ZODITCH

Yes.

TERENTIEVNA

And a sorrow it was when my master died, him being so sadly reduced in fortune.

(ZODITCH *stares at her for a moment and then resigns himself to the fact that she will not be silenced*)

SERGEY

He didn't have a kopeck what you could call his. And them what he owed money to was fierce.

TERENTIEVNA

There was always the moneylenders banging at the door of the house, but I never let none of them get at the master. I kept the doors locked in their faces I did, and I told them what they could do with their bills receivable. As God is my judge, mister, they woulda pulled the sheets off the bed he was dying on, if I'da let 'em, so vicious they was about getting their monies. What makes people get that way over money do you suppose, mister?

RUBIN

(*He speaks before* ZODITCH *has a chance to answer. He gestures at the painting of* MR. GRUBOV)

[ 13 ]

Well, what do you think, Mr. Zoditch, have they buried him yet?

(ZODITCH, *without answering, starts down the ladder*)

TERENTIEVNA

The master's house was what they called the Chulkaturin family house. (ZODITCH *looks at her*) Chulkaturin, mister. It's a name what nobody gets right, and him, poor soul, being the last of 'em what bore the name, who's to care now what the rights and wrongs of sounding it be?

RUBIN

Now that Mr. Grubov is tucked away, we can expect some changes wouldn't you say, Mr. Zoditch? (ZODITCH *still doesn't answer*) I'd imagine Mr. Pandalevski would be the man to watch.

(ZODITCH *sits down and begins adjusting himself. He removes the garters from his arms, pushes down his sleeves, runs his hand through his hair*)

TERENTIEVNA

And a hard thing it is to say "family house" when all that were near and dear to poor Mr. Chulkaturin, his mama and papa, was already gone and buried.

SERGEY

They was dead, wasn't they? Tell 'em about the rats.

TERENTIEVNA

During the winter I took service with the gentleman, I found the house overrun.

[ 14 ]

SERGEY

Rats big as horses' heads.

TERENTIEVNA

Not only rats, mister. Moles and other creature things what come burrowing in through the cellar to get in from the snow. He wouldn't let me drive them out, though I could have easy enough without him knowing because by that time he was near finished with this world, but I didn't have the heart to go against his wishes, him being perishing like he was and the doctor telling us to leave him be about the little things.

ZODITCH

Madam, I am not interested in rats, moles and medical reports.

SERGEY

And the lousy stream? What about that?

RUBIN

Of course the fact that Mr. Pandalevski accompanied Miss Grubov to the cemetery may not mean anything definite, unless it's a step in the right direction. A young girl has to rely on someone when her father's dead, don't you think?

(ZODITCH *starts angrily over to* RUBIN's *desk. He slams down a stack of manuscripts on it*)

ZODITCH

Work. Tweeze on your own time.

TERENTIEVNA

The boy is meaning a stream what belonged to the properties. When the master died the water went particularly bad.

[ 15 ]

SERGEY

It stank, that's what it did. And the garden had nothing to eat from it.


TERENTIEVNA

It was a flower garden, you see, mister.


SERGEY

Well, ya can't eat flowers, so what's the sense in that?


TERENTIEVNA

The flowers was particular treasured by him. You see, mister, he was a gentleman, which was why he didn't need to plant vegetables. And then after he died the spring came around again and everything was coming up, and that's a sorrow, him dead and everything coming up colorful.


RUBIN

Only who would have thought it would turn out to be Mr. Pandalevski she relied on. My money was on you, but he's a comer, he is. Well, it's all a ladder, Mr. Zoditch. It's up or it's down. We can't be keeping our feet on the same rung.


ZODITCH

Be still. I warn you. I'm the first reader.


TERENTIEVNA

The good Lord has his ways, I know, and none of us can choose the comings and goings of things, but I prayed for him that he would last through the spring so the flowers would give him pleasure.

[ 16 ]

SERGEY

So why didja pour the soapwater on 'em?


ZODITCH

Madam, I have already told you, you have come at a bad time. There has been a death in the firm.


TERENTIEVNA

(*Begins coughing. A very bad cough. She pulls out her handkerchief and spits into it*)
That clears it up, it does. So that's how it is with us, mister. All Mr. Chulkaturin left us in exchange for the cruel months of our services is what I got here. (*She takes a small parcel from her bag*) And it's for getting it made into a book with you bookmongers, which is what the gentleman himself was most insistent on so we could get paid something for our kindnesses to him, that me and the boy came to Petersburg. He didn't pay us a bit of wages so it's a fair thing we're doing now trying to make a little money off his writings, wouldn't you say, mister?

ZODITCH

Yes. Yes.

(*Annoyed, he takes the offered parcel*)


TERENTIEVNA

Not that I begrudge working for the sick. Doing a Christian duty to another fellow creature is doing no more than what Christ expects of us.

(ZODITCH *starts to unwrap the parcel. Suddenly there is the sound of a bell — the kind of bell that hangs over a door. Then the door slams shut*)

[ 17 ]

RUBIN

They're back.

(*There is a flurry of motion.* RUBIN *shoves his manicuring equipment into the desk and hurriedly begins reading and taking notes at the same time.* ZODITCH *puts on his coat. In come* MISS GRUBOV *and* MR. PANDALEVSKI. *They are dressed in black. As they pass by* ZODITCH, *he scurries out from behind his desk*)

ZODITCH

Miss Grubov. (PANDALEVSKI *and* MISS GRUBOV *stop.* ZODITCH *searches his pockets for an envelope and then remembers it is on his desk. He takes the envelope and hands it to* MISS GRUBOV) A note of condolence.

MISS GRUBOV

Thank you, Mr. Zoditch.

(*She starts to leave, but* ZODITCH *tries to get in a few more words while he has the opportunity.* PANDALEVSKI *frowns*)

ZODITCH

(*He speaks falteringly*)

I just wanted to say that I thought your father was wonderful, Miss Grubov, wonderful, a man to be admired, respected. It was an honor to be employed by him these past twelve years. We all miss him: a loss, a great loss . . .

MISS GRUBOV

Thank you.

(*Starts to go again. Again* ZODITCH *dribbles out a few words*)

ZODITCH

I hope it was not too cold for you, Miss Grubov. I thought of you in the carriage and I said they will forget the extra blankets. I . . . (*Starts backing away*) Excuse me. Excuse me.

MISS GRUBOV

It was fine in the carriage, Mr. Zoditch, thank you. (*She walks off stage*)

PANDALEVSKI

Bring up the tea to Miss Grubov. (*He starts to exit after* MISS GRUBOV *and then turns*) And a cup for me.

RUBIN

(*Although* PANDALEVSKI'S *words were spoken mostly to* ZODITCH, RUBIN *answers*)

Yes, Mr. Pandalevski. Right away. (*He starts out from behind his desk*)

ZODITCH

Where are you going? It is my privilege to bring up the tea. (RUBIN *just smiles and exits.* ZODITCH *runs after him*) Where do you think you're going? (*We hear him running down the steps after* RUBIN) It is my privilege.

(*As soon as* ZODITCH *leaves,* TERENTIEVNA *spits into the wastepaper basket. She opens her purse and, withdrawing a small flask, takes a quick snort.* SERGEY *begins hitting his boots*)

SERGEY

(*To boots*)

Damn you. Damn you. (*To* TERENTIEVNA) I don't like it here, grandma. I don't like him. I don't like anybody. (*Grabs his*

[ 19 ]

*boots and starts wringing them with his hands*) Arrrh, Arrrh, Arrrh. They're haunted. They're killing my feet. His ghost is in them. What's the sense in having boots to kill you? I don't want them. I told you to let him have his boots right from the beginning. (*Strikes boots again*) Arrrh. Arrrh. I don't feel well. Let's go to another bookmaker's place. You remember I wanted him to have his boots? You remember that? I don't like it here.

### TERENTIEVNA

Be still!

### SERGEY

Listen, I want a regular suit. While we're in Petersburg I want you to buy me a regular suit.

### TERENTIEVNA

You have a regular suit.

### SERGEY

This is not a regular suit. It hates me. It's his suit. His suit is not a regular suit. It doesn't fit me. The pants are too tight. Look how they make me walk. (*Gets up and walks as uncomfortably as possible. He keeps grabbing at the pants*) You see. Look. You see how I'm walking. They're tearing my legs to pieces. I can't put anything in the pockets. (*Flings himself back in the chair*) The jacket is crushing my chest. It cuts me under the arms. It twists my shoulders. Look at the collar. Do you see how tight it is? I can't breathe. Arrrh, Arrrh. Listen, you know what I think? (*Leans forward confidentially*) This was the suit Mr. Chulkaturin was meant to be buried in. Not the lousy one. This was the one he wanted. That's why it doesn't fit. It was supposed to go with him to the grave. I told you to let him take this suit. Let him take the good suit was what I said.

TERENTIEVNA

Be still!

SERGEY

I can't be still. It itches me. It chokes me. It tears my legs. It rubs my neck. It doesn't let me alone. Arrrh. Arrrh. (*Beats at the boots and tears them off*) Leave my feet alone, damn you. Damn you! (*Switches topic*) And when are we going to see the wild animals? I want to see the wild animals of Petersburg. You promised me. (*Again switching topic*) And maybe they won't buy his writings and then we won't make any money and then we've come all this way for what? For what? (*Rubbing his feet*) Arrrh. Arrrh. And then what? What about my yellow sled? What about that? Where's the money for that?

(ZODITCH *and* RUBIN *enter fighting over possession of a tea tray containing a tea pot, two cups, and a stack of biscuits*)

ZODITCH

It is my responsibility to bring the tea. Will you let go of it?

RUBIN

Mr. Pandalevski was talking to me.

ZODITCH

He was not, Mr. Rubin. He was talking to me. I have always brought the tea to Mr. Grubov and now I will bring it to Miss Grubov.

[ 21 ]

RUBIN

Will you let go? I am to bring the tea. He was talking to me.

ZODITCH

I am not going to let go. You let go. He was talking to me.
Don't be silly, Mr. Rubin.

RUBIN

I am not going to let go. I'm not being silly.

ZODITCH

Let go. You are being very silly.

RUBIN

No. It is you who are being very silly.

ZODITCH

You.

RUBIN

You.

ZODITCH

You.
   (*There is a real skirmish.* RUBIN *pulls the tray free with
a final jerk*)

RUBIN

You!
   (*He walks off stage.* ZODITCH *begins wandering about
the stage*)

[ 22 ]

TERENTIEVNA

(*Thinks this is a good time to continue her monologue*)

The master was a very refined type such as yourself, Mr. Zoditch, and he had a good handwriting, too, which comes from being so sensitive to things. You could tell he was delicate just from looking at his hands.

(ZODITCH *is at this moment in his pacing wringing his hands, and making almost animal noises in his frustration. He sits down on* RUBIN's *chair*)

ZODITCH

Madhouse. Madhouse. Up the ladder, is it?

(*He picks up a small bundle of* RUBIN's *pencils and breaks them*)

TERENTIEVNA

Yes, mister, a madhouse it is for sure, which is something of what the master said when he was trying to save the family properties which his father had gambled away. That was what they all said at the burial.

ZODITCH

(*Highly distracted, jumps up*)

Who said? Why do you go on and on? What are you talking about?

TERENTIEVNA

It was "they" what said it, mister. Those at the church what knew the family. They was coming and going in the law courts all the time, the mother and father was, and after the mother and father passed on, the poor gentleman continued fighting to save what was his. If you ask me it was the courts what drove him back and forth like a poor pigeon across the coun-

[ 23 ]

try. It was them what broke his heart. That was what done it, mister. The law stealing his property. Even down to the summer house which the law stole away from him for taxes. Didn't he get in a rage when he learnt that. (RUBIN *re-enters carrying the empty tea tray. He crosses over to his desk and, sitting on the edge of it, stares at* ZODITCH. ZODITCH *stares back at him furiously.* TERENTIEVNA *continues, trying to regain his attention*) You should have heard him, mister. "I won't have it. They won't get away with it," he says and such like, but they did get away with it. (*And then in a different tone of voice, as if what she now has to say has particular significance to* ZODITCH) Which is what they always do, ain't it, mister? The worst getting away with it all. (ZODITCH *looks back at her and they exchange a quiet stare.* TERENTIEVNA *then continues as before*) Oh, he was as much a fighter for things what was his as ever Death took away. He was never one to give up on things on account of him being a delicate soul. He was a brave sort and nobody can grudge him that. God love him for it.

### ZODITCH

So? So? You are finished? Eh? (*Angrily unwraps the parcel containing the MS and glances at it*) This is a diary. (*Pushes the MS back to* TERENTIEVNA. *Keeps looking over at* RUBIN, *off and on*) We do not publish diaries. You have talked all this time for nothing.

### TERENTIEVNA

Oh no, mister. It ain't a diary. It's papers.

### ZODITCH

It's a diary. (*Madly opens up to one of the pages and shoves it under her nose*) You see? March 20th? A day of the month. That's a diary.

[ 24 ]

TERENTIEVNA

No, mister. I can't read dates. Me and the boy can't read.
(*At this moment* MR. PANDALEVSKI *stands unseen at stage right, a cup of tea in his hand. Only* RUBIN *sees him.* RUBIN *gets instantly to work*)

ZODITCH

Well, I read dates, and it's a diary, madam. I assure you.
And I assure you that we do not read diaries, nor have we
ever in the entire history of the Grubov Publications published
one. So if you will excuse me . . .
(*When* ZODITCH *looks over toward* RUBIN *and sees* RUBIN *working, he imagines it is because he has asserted himself with* TERENTIEVNA, *and put* RUBIN *in his place. It fills him with renewed determination to be assertive. He keeps looking at* RUBIN)

TERENTIEVNA

You see, mister, it was just as a favor to the poor gentleman
what wrote it because he wanted to see us paid for our goods
and services that we come at all. He was a fine talker and word
writer.

ZODITCH

Oh, he was, was he?

SERGEY
(*To* TERENTIEVNA)

You're going to take me to see the wild animals of Petersburg!

[ 25 ]

ZODITCH

(*With mounting anger*)

A good writer was he? (*Whips open the pages of the diary*)
Well, he had a bad handwriting. How does that suit you? He
wrote with the hand of a pigmy. Tiny, tiny letters, too backward, too feminine. And where is the punctuation? Do you see
the punctuation? What has he done with that? Perhaps it is a
very long sentence and all the punctuation is at the end?
(*Turns the pages*) Ah, here is a comma. I have found a comma!
But where are the periods, the colons, the semi-colons, the
question marks? Where?

TERENTIEVNA

It's just writing, mister.

ZODITCH

Perhaps he has placed all his punctuation on the last page.
(*Turns to the last page*) No. I do not see them. In the middle,
perhaps they are stored in the middle. (*Turns to the middle*)
No. They are not in the middle. So I will shake the pages and
see if they fall out. (*Shakes the pages.* SERGEY *stares at the diary
and the floor as if he expects the punctuation to fall out*)

TERENTIEVNA

It's just writing, mister.

ZODITCH

There is no *just* writing! There is only proper and improper
writing. Your Mister Chulkaturin doesn't cross his t's, he ignores
his t's, he makes his t's look like l's, and the l's like b's, and the
b's like h's, and the h's like nothing at all. And why doesn't he

[ 26 ]

dot his i's? Why doesn't he loop his e's? I'll tell you why. Because he doesn't know anything: because he doesn't know how to write. We have here a babbling of consonants, a scribbling scribble, a disease that knows no punctuation, no sentencing, no paragraphing, a singular disease . . . (*At this point he sees* MR. PANDALEVSKI, *but he cannot stop. He would like to stop, but he goes on and on*) that rambles, that goes no place, that floats on streams of bombast, a leaking hulk of language in a sea of rhetoric, a babbling monument of incoherency . . . (*He rises in his chair until he stands*) a vacuum, a wasteland, a desert, a void, a . . . (*He stops. There is a moment of absolute silence, as* PANDALEVSKI *comes forward*)

PANDALEVSKI

Read it! Take it home with you, Mr. Zoditch. Read it!
(*Lights out*)
CURTAIN

# Scene Two

PLACE: ZODITCH's *apartment.*

TIME: *Early evening. Same day.*

SCENE: *The apartment is poorly furnished. It contains a coal stove, a desk, a bed, sundry other things.*

ON RISE: *The apartment is unoccupied. Outside the apartment, offstage right, we hear the shrill sounds of many small dogs barking. We next see* ZODITCH *hastening up the staircase. When he reaches the door to his room he stops and turns around.*

ZODITCH

(*Speaks out loud, although the words are directed towards himself*)

Bark your lungs out, you bitches. You think I'm afraid of your dogs, Katerina Prolomnaya. I'll take a stick to them. I'll beat their brains out. And where is the hall light, Katerina Prolomnaya? You are quick enough to ask for the rent.

(*The barking ceases.* ZODITCH *enters his room and, standing near the door, shouts into the hall*) There will be no rent without a hall light! (*Shuts door quickly. Barking immediately begins again. Offstage sound of a woman's voice,* KATERINA PROLOMNAYA, *the landlady*)

KATERINA
(*Offstage*)

Who opened his mouth? Show yourself! You miserable pack
of cowards. I'll set my dogs on ya, if I hear another word. You
hear me? It'll be a cold day in hell before Katerina Prolomnaya
takes garbage from the pack of you.
(*From somewhere in the darkened hall comes a feeble
voice*)

VOICE

No rent without a hall light!
(*This call is picked up by another voice, and then another, until there is a chorus of voices chanting one after
the other*)

VOICES

No rent without a hall light! No rent without a hall light!

KATERINA

No rent? A hall light? I'll throw the lot of you useless pieces
of baggage out on the street where you belong. I'm coming up.
(*Dogs bark louder. To tenants*) We'll see who it is that keeps
his door open now. (KATERINA *ascends the stairs. Sound of
doors shutting*) So you're shutting your doors, you crawling
pack of cowards. (*Stops right outside* ZODITCH'S *door. He is
plainly frightened*) Well, which one of you will stick his head
out now and ask me for it? Which one? (*Pause*) Which one?
(*She bursts into a laugh that echoes and re-echoes through the
halls of the house.* ZODITCH, *terribly frightened, keeps his back
against the door. Sounds of the dogs sniffing around, scratching at his door*) Come along Porshy, Potshy, Pinchy. (*Sound of

[ 29 ]

*the pack of them descending the stairs. Sound of her door shut-*
*ting, and then silence.*

 ZODITCH *goes over to his stove and looks inside. He takes*
*some paper and puts it in. He goes over to a small bucket*
*— the bucket has only a few pieces of coal in it. He spills*
*the entire amount into the stove and, striking a match,*
*lights it. He stands in front of it for a moment, rubbing his*
*hands. Then he picks up a pot of gruel which has been sit-*
*ting on the stove and takes it over to the desk. He reaches*
*into his pocket and pulls out the* CHULKATURIN *MS. He eats*
*while he talks* )

### ZODITCH

Take it home with you. Read it! I will not take it home with
me! I will not read it! Aagh. (*Slowly pronounces* CHULKATURIN'S
*name*) Chulkaturin. Mister Chulkaturin. You impossible name.
You gentleman. So much the worse for you if you believe
worms make distinctions underground. There are no distinctions underground. No better classes of worm. No gentleman's
worm. No worm with an uncommon body, an uncommon
mouth. You won't find them to your liking. I can assure you.
(*Takes a whiskey bottle out of his coat and a glass out of the*
*desk. Wipes the glass with his handkerchief. Pours in a tiny drop*
*and spends a few seconds savoring it and smacking his lips over*
*it*) Rest assured. Worms don't get down to boot level. You
won't get their tongue on your boot. They don't know about
the summer houses you had, your Mediterranean villas, your
ladies. Damn your ladies. Damn your fruits and peppermint
creams. Damn their parasols, their lawn parties, your fresh meat
and ice creams, your sailboats, your insolences. Aagh. (*Pours*
*out another tiny drop, and drinks it down the same way*) Here

you come to me. Down to me, and you satisfy me or I'll ship
you into oblivion. I'll take your bones and mangle them, I'll
break your head, I'll break your back. I'll . . .

(*In his anger he bends the spoon in his mouth.*

*All subsequent action, real or imagined, will be played
out within the room. The following is imagined*)

PANDALEVSKI

(*His voice comes from somewhere in the dark*)
Why don't you shut your mouth, you sack of hot air!

ZODITCH

(*Lights up on* PANDALEVSKI)
You scum. You garbage. You dregs. You horse's tail. Do not
think injustice goes unpunished. Do not think this is the office.
Here there is freedom. Here you watch what you say to me.
A trip to the cemetery does not make a love affair. Keep your
hands off my water jug.

PANDALEVSKI

(*Pours the water from the jug into a basin*)
On the trip to the cemetery it was boringly obvious which
direction the affection of Miss Grubov lay. Spreading the blan-
ket to cover our legs from the chill, I found that by a subtle
snaky motion of her torso she connived it so that one two three
our thighs and hips were dancing flank to flank to the rolling
of the wheels. Hand me the soap.

ZODITCH

Who do you think you're ordering about? I am the head of
the reader's section, the first reader, you carbuncle, you wart,

[ 31 ]

you pimple. I do not take orders from you. I will dance on your grave before I'm through.

PANDALEVSKI

Hardly had this dance begun when by a writhing of her arm, a heaving breathing of her bosom, as if the desire in her must burst, she seized my fingers one by one and locked them in the compass of her hand. Get me the soap!

ZODITCH

I'm warning you, Pandalevski. Watch what you say. Do not push me too far. Be careful. I will not put up with these lies.

PANDALEVSKI

Seizing thus my hand, she covered it with kisses and sent it, as it were, on a foreign exploration to private lands best left undiscovered outside the marriage bed. I pretended fright, surprise, but her importunities and protestations were of such severe necessity I at last gave way and exposed her bosom. Get me the soap!

ZODITCH

You liar! You defamer! What right do you have to say such things?

PANDALEVSKI

The soap!

ZODITCH

The soap is it? (*Reaches over and grabs the soap bar*) Here is the soap. (*He brings the bar of soap down on top of* PANDALEVSKI's *hat and proceeds to hammer* PANDALEVSKI *into the ground*) I'll drive you into the ground. I'll beat your brains out.

[ 32 ]

We'll see who's whose superior. We'll see about trips to the cemetery, you carcass, you liar, you buzzard, you ink pot. (ZODITCH *drags* PANDALEVSKI *to the door and out.* PANDALEVSKI *holds on to his hat*) Down the stairs with you! (*Curiously enough there is no barking from the dogs.* ZODITCH *returns and stands by the door*) Monstrous liar. Vilifier. What right to say such things?

(*The voice of* PANDALEVSKI *is heard from the direction of the washbasin. He is lathering his hands with soap*)

#### PANDALEVSKI

What right to say such things? Once having seduced Miss Grubov, once having aroused in her the fevered breath of passion, which I found most sour to the smell, I suppose I have all rights to say what pleases me. Hand me the towel. (ZODITCH *doesn't move*) It was then that I thrust your name into the conversation where it fell like a small stone dropped from some low height into the sea. "And what of Zoditch," I said, and when there was no sign of recognition on the lady's lips, I pressed forward with encouragements to her remembrance: "The rude fellow, the crude fellow, the open the door and 'if you please,' fellow, the tea fellow, the biscuit fellow, the a b c and loop your e's fellow." But there was no remembrance. You are, nevertheless, welcome to the wedding along with the bookkeeper and the printer's apprentice. Hand me the towel.

#### ZODITCH

There will be no wedding!

#### PANDALEVSKI

Oh, yes, a very large wedding. Hand me the towel!

ZODITCH

There will be no wedding. She is untouched.

PANDALEVSKI

I have washed my fingers, have I not? Do I wash my fingers for no reason? Hand me the towel!

ZODITCH

I'll give you the towel. (*Takes the towel and suddenly wraps it around* PANDALEVSKI'S *throat. There is a struggle this time*) Sleep with the devil in hell tonight. Enough of your insults. Your lies. Enough. Enough. (PANDALEVSKI *slumps to the floor.* ZODITCH *nudges him a few times to make sure he is dead*) It is finished. Idiot! (*He drags* PANDALEVSKI *out, returns. He sits at his desk once again. He spoons in his gruel*)

Was it too cold, Miss Grubov? I thought of you in the carriage and I said they will forget the extra blankets and Miss Grubov will be cold. It's a long drive to any cemetery and the horses move so slowly.

(*Following is imagined*)

MISS GRUBOV

(*From the dark. Her voice flat, almost as if hypnotized*)
Yes, it was cold.

(*As she speaks the light goes up revealing her seated on* ZODITCH'S *bed*)

ZODITCH

(*Still eating*)

That is too bad. In the winter when Death comes to Petersburg, he takes the large and the small: I have heard forty to fifty cats, their eyes like jelly ice, their whiskers stiff as banjo

[ 34 ]

wire, die each night. I have heard a like number of cur-bitches
with teats so locked with rime they could not suck their puppies
die each night. I have heard birds innumerable die each night
seeking warmth in chimney smoke — and I thought of you huddled in the carriage, your father before you, his great black
coat wrapped about him and his eyes shut to eternity come,
and I said she will listen to the horses kicking up the ice and
she will know in her heart she is alone.

(*He stands up and wipes his mouth with the back of his
hand. Goes thru his obsequies: rubs shoes against pants,
wets fingers and runs them up and down trouser crease,
cleans wax out of ears, slicks down hair*)

MISS GRUBOV

I sat in the chapel with my father, and the cold sunlight
shone over the length of his body and I was alone.

ZODITCH

(*Stands by her side and begins unbuttoning her jacket*)
There was loneliness.

MISS GRUBOV

I was alone. Lonely.

ZODITCH

What were you thinking of?

MISS GRUBOV

I thought of nothing. I saw nothing.

ZODITCH

(*Begins ravishing her*)
Without me, nothing. Nothing. (*She responds and they embrace on the bed*) I am to be promoted.

[ 35 ]

MISS GRUBOV

Yes, I will promote you.

ZODITCH

I will fire Pandalevski. I will set my desk in the main office.
I will be served tea and I will have what is mine to have. I will
buy a sailboat. I will buy a house. I will buy a carriage to go
to the operas.

MISS GRUBOV

Yes. Yes. You shall have all.

ZODITCH

I love you.

MISS GRUBOV

Marry me. Marry.

ZODITCH

Yes. Yes. Yes. Yes. Yes. (*They embrace for a few seconds. Suddenly* RUBIN *appears. He watches them for a second or two and
then, bending down, picks* ZODITCH *up by the seat of his pants
and the scruff of his neck and tosses him to the floor*) You! You!
You! You!

(RUBIN *is already in the bed on top of* MISS GRUBOV.
ZODITCH *tries to grapple with* RUBIN *but* RUBIN *shoves him
to the floor with his foot.* ZODITCH *remains on the floor.*
MISS GRUBOV *speaks as she engages in lovemaking with*
RUBIN. *They roll from side to side in the bed. They laugh*)

RUBIN

It's all a ladder, Mr. Zoditch. We can't be keeping our feet on
the same rung, can we?

[ 36 ]

MISS GRUBOV

There are matters that have come to my attention, Mr. Zoditch.

ZODITCH

(*Scurrying over to the bed*)

What matters?

MISS GRUBOV

Complaints that may lead to your dismissal.

ZODITCH

This is impossible. Your father promised to advance me. I have told everybody I am to be advanced.

MISS GRUBOV

My father is dead. Death causes change.

ZODITCH

There can be no change in this. I have served with loyalty for twelve years.

MISS GRUBOV

Those who have watched you say you seek a strange advancement.

ZODITCH

They are madmen. You must not believe their lies.

MISS GRUBOV

Do they lie?

ZODITCH

They lie. Dear Miss Grubov believe me. I think of you only
as a person above me. I do not dream. I'm not a man driven
by dreams. You don't know them. How they connive. How they
watch me to discover evil. They distort me. They twist me into
shapes I am not. It is they who harbor these evils. Yes. It is
they. I can give you their names.

MISS GRUBOV

Can you?

ZODITCH

Yes. Yes. It is the man in the bookkeeping section, and the
printer's apprentice. You see? I know them. I spit on them.
They do not respect your virginity. They make jokes. It is they
who seek strange advancement.

(MISS GRUBOV *and* RUBIN *laugh and throw the covers over
themselves*)

ZODITCH

Do not treat me this way, Miss Grubov. I am a man of feeling. I am not a nothing. I am a man of respect, of sentiments.
(*They just continue to make love*) Stop it. You have no right
to do this. Stop it. Stop it. What do you think I am? You think
I am a toad! I am a man to be respected. Everybody in this
house comes to me because I am a man of influence. This is my
bed! (*Once again he is pushed away from the bed by the feet
of* RUBIN *and* MISS GRUBOV. *He falls to the floor and yells from
the floor*) You think there were not affairs I had? What do you
know of that? There were women who loved me. When I was
not even twenty there was a woman who wanted to marry me,

[ 38 ]

who said I was handsome. She thought I was a soldier. (*The muted sounds under the covers have become increasingly animalistic.* ZODITCH *speaks in a calmer tone as he returns to his desk*) I could have been an officer, but there was no one to speak for me.

(*Lights out on bed.* ZODITCH *slumps down at his desk and opens* CHULKATURIN's *diary*)

I would have been a captain by now.

(*As* ZODITCH *silently reads, the lights come up on* CHULK-ATURIN *standing near the bed*)

#### CHULKATURIN

I, Nikolai Alexeevich Chulkaturin, in my twenty-ninth year, certain in the hope of the resurrection and the life to come, begin this my diary at Lambswater, March the twentieth, eighteen seventy.

#### ZODITCH

(*Still thinking of his own problems, calls out*)
I had no one to speak for me!

#### CHULKATURIN

The doctor, the same doctor that brought me into this world, came this morning with his black bag of useless medicines to tell me that I must now prepare myself to be shortly ushered out of it. At the end of all his medical subterfuges and hem-hawing terminologies he told me only what I already knew — I am to die. So be it. My life has been as brief as it has been meaningless, and death's a goodness for all we know.

(*Lights up on* DR. KORVIN *standing near the bed*)

[ 39 ]

DOCTOR

I will leave this here for you, Nikolai. (*Places a bottle on the night table*) If you are troubled by pain you are to take a teaspoonful. In any event have a teaspoonful before you retire. It will assure you a good night's sleep. It's opium. If you dream, do not pay any attention to it.

CHULKATURIN

(*Speaking as if to himself*)

This morning I dreamt I was in a great cage in some marketplace I had never seen before. The sun burned down upon me and I could not escape. I kept sticking my hand through the bars of the cage, grasping at those who passed by, but they would not stop and I had lost all power to speak. I could not breathe. I felt myself suffocating, and no person stopped.

(*He turns to look at the Doctor as if expecting an explanation*)

DOCTOR

I will have that Terentievna of yours open the window a crack before you retire this evening. (SERGEY, *without knocking, opens the door a trifle and sticks his head in.* CHULKATURIN *lies down on the bed*) Oh, there you are. It's about time. What took you so long?

SERGEY

I was chasing the cats away.

DOCTOR

Away from what? (SERGEY *just shrugs his shoulders*) Well, come in, come in. There are some sheets in the closet I want you to take down to your grandmother to wash.

[ 40 ]

SERGEY
(*Pointing to the closet*)
In here?

DOCTOR
Yes. Be quick about it. (SERGEY *opens the closet and looks at all the clothes before he bends down to pick up the sheets. He suddenly backs away, letting out a cry*) What's the matter with you?

SERGEY
There's blood on 'em.

DOCTOR
Never mind what's on them. Just take them down to your grandmother. (SERGEY *picks up the sheets with great distaste and leaves*) Stupid lout. If your father were alive he'd pick them both up by the neck and toss them out.

ZODITCH
(*Interrupting with a comment. Action freezes*)
I'll pick you up by the neck and toss you out!

DOCTOR
(*Action resumes*)
Do you know what she was doing when I came in this morning? Sleeping! Big as you please, sprawled out in bed with a bottle of vodka clutched to her chest and her legs dangling to the floor. She's allowed the downstairs to become a rat's den.

CHULKATURIN
Terentievna's old and she drinks, but she is here when I need her. The boy is somewhat backward. Everyday he sticks his

head into the room to see that I have not made off with the closet. He fancies my clothes.

DOCTOR

And the old woman? What does she fancy?

CHULKATURIN

The house.

DOCTOR

Look here, Nikolai, this is none of my affair, but if you do not watch what you are doing they will rob the teeth out of your head before they are done. Do not underestimate the cunning of poor people. You do not know them.

CHULKATURIN

(*Seriously*)

I have never known anybody, Doctor Korvin. (*Changing mood*) But do not worry, nothing is settled yet. We negotiate day by day. Besides, to whom else should these clothes and this house belong? By the time I am gone she will have earned this roof over her head.

DOCTOR

And the summer house? What has become of that?

CHULKATURIN

Sold at auction. A cloth merchant from Novgorod. A man who had to have a summer house.

DOCTOR

This is all quite distressing to hear, Nikolai. Surely, some other alternative presented itself to you.

[ 42 ]

CHULKATURIN

No, doctor. Let the summer house be gone. What it meant to my father, it never meant to me and for it the Chulkaturins, father and son, are at last quits with the human race. I have paid off the last of my father's obligations and if no man will be the richer for the Chulkaturins having lived, well, no man can say he is the poorer either. Do not look so concerned, Doctor Korvin. Obligations must be met.

DOCTOR

Your friends will not permit this, Nikolai. To sell your property this way is demeaning. You are no merchant's son.

CHULKATURIN

I have no friends, doctor.

DOCTOR

You have had friends, Nikolai. At the university I'm sure you made many friends. (*There is no answer from* CHULKATURIN *so the* DOCTOR *makes his own*) Every man has friends.

(*The* DOCTOR *busies himself putting back his medicines and collecting together his odds and ends. He pays no attention to* CHULKATURIN)

CHULKATURIN

Upon meeting my friends on the street of the university: "Why it's Chulkaturin," they say, and when I approach, the circle of friends parts as if a slightly leprous thing had been thrust into their midst. And the eyes which had been set upon my eyes begin dropping from my face to my chest to my knees to the bottom of my feet, and everybody stands absolutely struck-still desperately trying to remember what it was they were saying before I arrived. Once I am ten feet past, the circle once again shrinks, the eyes once more rise, and conversation moves like fish hustling down the Don. Oh Christ, that the circles of this world might shrink and find me standing locked inside!

(*Unaware of what* CHULKATURIN *has said, the* DOCTOR *turns to him*)

DOCTOR

Try not to have too many visitors, Nikolai . . . You must get your rest.

CHULKATURIN

Doctor? I'll see that you are paid as soon as I can.

(*The* DOCTOR *exits as* TERENTIEVNA *comes in, broom in hand*)

TERENTIEVNA

He's a bit of nose, ain't he? He was staring into everything downstairs when he first come. Even poked into my room and me with a bottle of furniture polish in my hand at the time and the dress about the knees from bending over.

CHULKATURIN

I'm sure he meant nothing by it, Terentievna. He used to visit this house often when my parents were alive.

TERENTIEVNA

I'm not a housekeeper to have her work looked after by them what ain't of the family. I do my job.

CHULKATURIN

Yes, I'm sure you do.

TERENTIEVNA

I do my dusting and my window washing and my floor cleaning and my cooking and them what ain't of the family has other
business to mind. (CHULKATURIN *reaches over to take his writing pad and pencil out of the night table*) Let them stick their
noses to their own face.

CHULKATURIN

Terentievna, there is something you can do for me.

TERENTIEVNA

And what would that be?

CHULKATURIN

I'm going to do some writing and when I am finished I want
you to promise me that you will take it downstairs to the
kitchen stove and burn it.

TERENTIEVNA

Burn it, sir?

CHULKATURIN

Yes. You are not to show it to anybody, or get anybody's advice about what to do with it. You will take it straight to the
stove, you understand?

TERENTIEVNA

Is it letters, sir?

[ 45 ]

CHULKATURIN

No. Just writing that I wish to do for myself. Just a whim, it will be of no value or concern to anyone, so it is to be destroyed.

TERENTIEVNA

Yes, sir.

CHULKATURIN

You will do this without fail, Terentievna?

TERENTIEVNA

That I will. Is it bad news the doctor was bringing about the cough, then?

CHULKATURIN

Yes.

TERENTIEVNA

The cough's not to go away?

CHULKATURIN

No, Terentievna, it will not go away.

TERENTIEVNA

I'm sorry for that, sir, truly I am.

CHULKATURIN

I know you are, Terentievna.

TERENTIEVNA

It's the good what always go before us and the bad what come dragging after. It's a bad world, sir, that's what it is, and none of us can look for justice in it. (*Pause, and then slyly*) Is it soon you'll be leaving us, sir?

CHULKATURIN

I don't know, Terentievna. (*She nods her head up and down as if thinking something over*) Is there something else?

TERENTIEVNA

No, sir, only . . . well, it's the boots and the clothes in the closet. I was wondering if you'd be wearing them again.

CHULKATURIN
(*Softly*)

No.

TERENTIEVNA

Sir?

CHULKATURIN

You can have them, Terentievna.

TERENTIEVNA

You see, it's for the boy. He doesn't have much in the way of shoes fit for the snow and all, and him without a winter coat . . .

CHULKATURIN

Yes. You are right. There is no need to wait.

TERENTIEVNA

(*Goes to the closet and pulls out the boots and winter coat*)

[ 47 ]

We'll be obliged to you for this kindness, sir. You're a gentleman what understands.

CHULKATURIN

Those were my father's boots, Terentievna.

TERENTIEVNA

Yes, sir, and fine leather they are, too. Would the overcoat
be your father's, too?

CHULKATURIN

No.

TERENTIEVNA

It's hardly worn at all, is it? It's the changing of the styles
what do it for gentlemen more than the wearing of them out,
I suppose. There are some what get a new coat every year just
for the new look of it, they say. Will we be needing the services
of a lawyer, sir?

CHULKATURIN

For what?

TERENTIEVNA

The house, sir. Can we make our agreements by the speaking
of them, or do we have to have them writ down by the lawyers?

CHULKATURIN

They must be written down.

TERENTIEVNA

Oh, must they? Everything is a fuss, ain't it?

[ 48 ]

CHULKATURIN

You can tell Sergey to fetch Lawyer Levinov tomorrow. I will have him draw up the transfer papers.

TERENTIEVNA

Yes, sir. And don't you trouble yourself about anything. I don't mind at all about the sheets. I'm going to do the wash right now.

CHULKATURIN

You won't pour the washwater in the stream, will you, Terentievna? I don't want the carp and grudgeon killed by the soap.

TERENTIEVNA

Don't you worry about that, sir. Don't you worry. I'll find another place.

(*Exits. Lights dim to indicate a passage of time*)

CHULKATURIN

March twenty-second. Lawyer Levinov came yesterday and as I signed the papers giving the house over to Terentievna upon my death, I felt that by that simple signature I had somehow set myself irrevocably free: as a piece of ice that has been bound all winter flows at last down to the sea, so I too have become unbound. To flow where? God knows.

(*Lights up on* LEVINOV)

LEVINOV

I find myself hard put to even describe the coach ride over. The driver, a lunatic of a fellow, was absolutely insensitive to anything other than meeting his schedule. Although the four horses we had were good and we were flying along, this madman insisted on adding a fifth horse. This poor horse was completely out of place, completely superfluous. (*Points to a spot on the page*) Sign there, too, Mr. Chulkaturin. (*He continues with his story*) And how was this unnecessary horse fastened to the carriage? Absolutely all wrong. By means of a short thick rope that constantly cut into his flank so that his flesh was at all times positively lacerated. How he expected the beast to run naturally when its entire body was arched in pain I don't know. And what was this lunatic's reaction when I informed him that we would do better without this superfluous horse? (*Points to another spot*) And here as well, Mr. Chulkaturin. (*Continues with the story*) He began lashing the horse, a dozen additional strokes across its back and swollen belly, and screaming out to the wind. "What the hell. It's been tied on, and if not to run then what the hell for?"

(CHULKATURIN *and lawyer stare at each other. Lights out on* LEVINOV. ZODITCH *flips a page*)

#### CHULKATURIN

March twenty-third. Sunday. The church bells have been ringing all morning, heavy, slow, melodious, and so they will ring when I am no longer here to listen. I cannot bear to hear them. I have had Terentievna shut the window tight, but still the sound washes into the empty room filling every corner. In darkness I see the meadow where once I played, the branches of my plum tree bending with fruit, the small streams where I caught carp. Oh my Christ, if I cannot say good-bye to the summers that warmed me, the winters I put my fur hat on to! If I cannot say good-bye, what shall I do? Who will have pity for us all?

(ZODITCH *runs over to the bed.* CHULKATURIN *stares frozenly ahead*)

[ 50 ]

ZODITCH

Pity? Why do you waste my time with pity? There is no pity. Up the ladder. Down the ladder. Make up your mind to it. Do not live in the delusion you will put tears in my eyes. In me you do not deal with an amateur of suffering. (*Mimics* CHULKA-TURIN) "The church bells have been ringing all morning." Let them ring! Every bell rings; every dog cries; every sheep bleats tears. The public is not interested in suffering. In me you deal with the public, Chulkaturin. Who is to buy the lungs and brains of you, that is what I am to decide. That is why I am a first reader. That . . . (*Finally becomes aware of a slight but persistent knocking on his door. Lights out on* CHULKATURIN. ZODITCH *goes over to his door*) Who is it?

FEATHERS

It's me, sir, the housegirl, Feathers.

ZODITCH

(*Opens the door*)

What do you want?

FEATHERS

(*A young girl, filthy from coal dust and in rags. She smiles constantly, nervously*)

Katerina Prolomnaya sent me with a bucket of coal.

ZODITCH

(*Imitates her*)

Katerina Prolomnaya sent me with a bucket of coal. (*Lets her in. Harshly*) Well, don't stand there smiling all night. I've important work that must be done. We can't all afford to live like princesses.

[ 51 ]

FEATHERS

Shall I put the coal in the stove for you, Mr. Zoditch?

ZODITCH

(*With a wave of his hand indicates she is to do so*)
Yes. Why have you brought the coal to all the others and only now to me? Why am I the last? I won't forget that, Miss Feathers.

FEATHERS

Oh, no, sir. You're not the last. The mistress says the others aren't to have any coal at all tonight, only you, sir. She says let 'em freeze and the city would be better off without them.

ZODITCH

Do not give me stories. Coal doesn't grow on plum trees, madam! I do not live in fairy tales. (FEATHERS *busies herself putting the coal in the stove*) She expects something for this, eh? Eh? What does she expect? Nobody does anything without expectations. If she expects to be paid now, I cannot pay now. To be advanced in the publishing business is not to be made a prince. I didn't ask for any extra coal.

FEATHERS

The mistress said nothing about asking for money, sir.

ZODITCH

Nothing? What nothing? You watch what you're doing there. You're putting in too much at once. You're not dealing with a spendthrift, Miss Feathers.

[ 52 ]

FEATHERS

And I was to bring you this kerosene, sir.
(*She hands him the kerosene. He just stares at it*)

ZODITCH

Why? (*Hesitantly takes it and, opening the jar, sticks his nose to it to make sure it's what she says it is*) She expects to make up on the coal by overcharging me on the oil. That's it, isn't it? Well, I will not pay a kopeck for the oil. I will not pay for the coal. I asked for nothing and from nothing comes nothing. I do not need these extravagances.

FEATHERS

The mistress said nothing about money for the kerosene, sir.

ZODITCH

Tell Katerina Prolomnaya I cannot afford extravagances . . . I live close to the bone. Do something about that smile! (*Ushers* FEATHERS *out and locks the door. Once again he smells the kerosene*) Is she so rich that she can give something for nothing. Rich? From what, rich? Her husband died owing the moneylenders. Everybody knows he died owing the moneylenders. (*Stands in front of the mirror and stares at himself. He runs his hands through his hair and preens a little*) But if he didn't die owing the moneylenders. If . . . Bah!
(*Turns from the mirror. Picks up the diary and begins reading. Immediately there is a stabbing cry of pain that comes from* CHULKATURIN *in bed. Lights come up dimly.* CHULKATURIN's *arm extends itself opening and closing as if seeking to grasp onto* ZODITCH. *The* DOCTOR *steps out of the shadows*)

[ 53 ]

DOCTOR

So, Nikolai, so. What has happened is a certain flow of blood from the lung. You understand? Now we must engage in the removal of a like quantity of blood. You will feel better after you are bled. It is to be expected that spittle from the lungs, since the hemorrhage, will be somewhat pasty, like clay, even like clay. A slight disruption of the digestive organs, the increased frequency of intestinal discharge in turn brings about an additional grabbing and uncontracting, as it were, of the bowels, which in turn produces the diarrhea. Do not distress yourself with keeping your sheets clean. That is nothing to distress yourself about. A trifle of blood, a trifle of excrement. You understand? So. So.

(*Lights out on* DOCTOR *and* CHULKATURIN)

ZODITCH

(*Nervously*)

Who's to say what handsome is? Katerina Prolomnaya's first husband was short. What was Napoleon if not short, or Caesar? *Veni, vidi, vici.* It is a medical fact that the short man, by having his heart placed closer to his brain, enjoys a richer supply of blood, ergo, a proportionate enlargement of the cranial area so that he becomes quicker in wit, more active in deed, greater in accomplishment. To marry Katerina Prolomnaya would be a diminishment . . .

(*He begins biting at his nail, and then laughing and then biting and then laughing. Glances at MS.*

*Lights up on* DOCTOR *as he pours a beaker of* CHULKATURIN's *blood into* ZODITCH's *washbasin. Lights out on* DOCTOR. *Lights up on* CHULKATURIN *in bed. He is writing*)

[ 54 ]

CHULKATURIN

Think, dear Christ, have you made me anything more than Lawyer Levinov's fifth horse? If I had never lived it would have made no difference to anyone. My entire existence has been superfluous. That is the central fact of my being: the central word that sums up my total meaning. Think, dear Christ, is that not so? Have you not made me a fifth horse fastened uselessly to the coach of life? To whose benefit do I run? For whose benefit am I beaten? Oh my Christ, where is my posthouse?

(*Action freezes.* CHULKATURIN *looks straight ahead*)

ZODITCH

So it is a husband she is after. She sends Miss Chimney Sweep with the kerosene to keep me from getting an eyestrain. Five feet four inches can hardly be considered short in any event. She doesn't wish me to be eyestrained because she is concerned. The coal alone might be construed as meaning no more than a mere landlord-tenant relationship. So if she just sent the coal she might expect no more than a thank you, but more than a thank you is floating around here. The time I left my gloves on the hall table and she called out to me on the street: "Oh, Mr. Zoditch, your gloves." And the payment of the rent, did she not say, "Ah, Mr. Zoditch, your rent." What was the "Ah" about? "Ah, Mr. Zoditch." Ahs and ohs have meanings. They don't just blow around the air! One does not say "ah" . . . "oh" just for the pleasure of opening a mouth. (*Begins biting his fingernails again and looking at himself in the mirror*) Surely she loved me even while her husband was alive! (*Does a stupid little jig. Begins to read*)

CHULKATURIN

April the second, Wednesday. It rains now. A cold soundless rain that falls into the snow and vanishes. I struggle to separate the days one from the other. It is useless. I think of you, Liza, my rainbow, my bird, caught now forever fixed in the timeless grace of your seventeen years, and I know as truly as I must have known all these years that in you and in you alone exists all I shall ever know of useless happiness, and useless agony. Now I begin. Now at the end of my life I prove, dear God, that had I never lived it would have made no difference to anyone. (*Takes a slight pause before continuing*) Some years ago, I was obliged to spend some months in a small town lying in one of the more remote districts — a town overrun by mud and goats. Fortunately, the parents of Illya Ozhogin, an acquaintance I had known for a single term at the University, lived there, and before I found myself desperate with boredom, I resolved to pay a call. I sent a boy from the inn I was lodged at, to announce my arrival to the Ozhogins.

(*Lights out on* CHULKATURIN. *Scene with the* OZHOGINS *becomes animated. Light remains on* ZODITCH. KIRILLA MATVEICH OZHOGIN *sits with his hands folded on his belly.* ANNA, *his wife, is sewing.* BIZMIONKOV, *the family friend, plays a game of solitaire.* LIZA *toys with a caged bullfinch.* ZODITCH *identifies the characters in* CHULKATURIN's *story with people familiar to him in his own life. Thus:* KIRILLA MATVEICH *is* MR. GRUBOV, *the man in the portrait at the publishing house;* BIZMIONKOV *is* PANDALEVSKI; LIZA *is* MISS GRUBOV)

KIRILLA

(*Pulling a watch from his vest and looking at it*)
If he's going to call, why doesn't he call? And why isn't the

dinner ready yet? It's already after twelve. How much longer must we wait to eat? Liza, go into the kitchen and find out what they're doing there. (LIZA, *busy playing with the bull-finch, doesn't hear*) Elizaveta!

LIZA

Yes, papa?

KIRILLA

Go into the kitchen and find out what the delay is. (*She can scarcely tear herself away from the bird. She exits staring at the bird all the way*) That girl is turning deaf, positively. And crazy, as well. All day with that bird. (*Imitates* LIZA *with the bird*) Eech. Eech, eech. Ooooch. Ooooch. Eech, eech.

BIZMIONKOV

(*Calmly continuing with his game*)

It is the same with all young girls, Kirilla Matveich. There is nothing to be concerned about.

KIRILLA

We will see if you sing the same tune, my friend, when you marry and have a daughter who arranges flowers all day and tickles bullfinches. Maybe you should marry my Liza and then we will see what you say.

(ANNA *offers one of her little social laughs*)

KIRILLA

(*Pulling out his watch again*)

Is he coming for lunch, or what?

[ 57 ]

BIZMIONKOV

*(Calmly)*

When you send a messenger at lunchtime, you are coming for lunch.

ANNA

I'll have them set another place.

*(Leaves excitedly)*

KIRILLA

Don't get rich, Bizmionkov. Take my advice. Stay poor. When you live in poverty, you live in happiness. Your meals are served on time.

BIZMIONKOV

Money is a curse.

(LIZA *returns*)

KIRILLA

Liza, dear, go back into the kitchen and get a little snack to hold Mr. Bizmionkov over to lunch.

BIZMIONKOV

I can wait for lunch, there is no need to go to extra effort.

KIRILLA

There is no need starving yourself, my friend. Why be a martyr? If we have to wait for Mr. Chulka . . . Chulkaturin, we have to wait, but there is no need to starve. We are not at the gates of starvation here. Just bring some fish, Liza . . . *(She keeps starting out, but his additional requests keep calling her back)* . . . with lemon . . . bread . . . some olives . . .

five or six . . . better bring the same for me . . . some kvass to drink . . . you want some kvass, Bizmionkov? (BIZMIONKOV *nods.* LIZA *has started toying with the bullfinch again*) Some kvass for Mr. Bizmionkov, too. Eh? What, are you playing with that bird again? Leave the bird alone. (LIZA *exits back to the kitchen.* KIRILLA *looks after her to make sure she is gone*) Listen, Bizmionkov, I have something I want to talk to you about.

(KIRILLA *tries to start, but isn't quite sure how to frame his remarks*)

### BIZMIONKOV

Well?

### KIRILLA

It's about Liza. (*Still hesitates*) When you're a father you notice things.

### BIZMIONKOV

Yes?

### KIRILLA

Don't rush me.

### BIZMIONKOV

Who is rushing you?

### KIRILLA

As I was saying, you notice things when you're a father.

### BIZMIONKOV

What things?

### KIRILLA

What do you mean, "what things?" Things! What I want to know is what kind of a bird is that?

[ 59 ]

BIZMIONKOV

(*Going up to the bird*)

A bullfinch. What else would it be? You thought it was an owl?

KIRILLA

I know it's a bullfinch, but what kind of a bullfinch?

BIZMIONKOV

A Russian bullfinch.

KIRILLA

A female? Is it a female?

BIZMIONKOV

What difference does it make what sex it is? Isn't it singing all right?

KIRILLA

Will you look under the feathers and stop asking a thousand questions.

BIZMIONKOV

It won't raise its tail.

KIRILLA

Wait a minute.

(*He opens the cage and starts to stick his hand in just as his wife comes in*)

ANNA

What are you doing?

[ 60 ]

KIRILLA

(*Quickly pulling out his hand*)

Nothing. I was merely placing my hand in the bird's cage.


BIZMIONKOV

Kirilla Matveich wants to know if the bird is a male or a . . .

KIRILLA

Sha. (*To wife*) Nothing. It is nothing.


ANNA

Isn't it singing well?

KIRILLA

It is singing well. I just felt like feeling its feathers, that's all. Have you set another place for our son's friend?


ANNA

Yes.

KIRILLA

Well, let's not stand in front of the bird's cage all day. (*Return to seats.* KIRILLA *makes a big production about sitting down.* ANNA *eyes him suspiciously*) Ah! My favorite chair. (*Nobody says anything. To wife*) Are you going to be sitting there for a while, Anna?


ANNA

Is there some reason I should not sit here?


KIRILLA

No reason. Of course there's no reason.


ANNA

Then I will be sitting here for a while.

[ 61 ]

KIRILLA

There is nothing further that needs your attention in the kitchen?

ANNA

What else should need my attention in the kitchen?

KIRILLA

I don't know, Anna. I was only asking. (*Pause*) Things do not go well all the time in the kitchen, that is all. (ANNA *gets up*) Where are you going?

ANNA

Back to the kitchen.

KIRILLA

If things are going well there is no need to go back to the kitchen. (ANNA *starts to return to her chair*) But if you feel it needs your attention . . .

(ANNA *leaves the room, almost tearfully.* KIRILLA *hastens over to the cage and, opening the little door, sticks his hand in*)

ANNA

(*Returns unexpectedly.* KIRILLA's *hand gets momentarily caught in the cage*)

If the meal is not right, it is not my fault. I do my best. (*Almost in anguish*) What do you want from that little bird?

KIRILLA

(*Exasperated*)

Nothing. We are going into the garden. Come, my friend, come, come. Why must you exasperate me so, Anna.

(*Takes* BIZMIONKOV's *arm and escorts him out of the room.* ANNA, *still distraught, exits — passing her daughter*

[ 62 ]

*who has just entered with a tray.* LIZA *puts the tray down
and stands looking about her for a second. Then, for no
apparent reason, she whirls about the room ending up in
front of the bird cage. She dances about the cage and
begins whistling to the bird. There is a knock at the door,
which brings* LIZA *out of her little trance. She looks about
her for a second and then seeing that there is no one to
answer she goes to the door.* CHULKATURIN *comes in. He is
rather overdressed, almost foppish, somehow ill at ease.
He tends to make little mistakes in manners due to his
anxiety)*

CHULKATURIN

Excuse me, I am Nikolai Alexeevich Chulkaturin.

LIZA

I am Elizaveta Kirillovna, Illya's sister.
         (*They just stand looking at each other*)

CHULKATURIN

Is there anything wrong? I sent a messenger to say that I
was to follow.

LIZA

Oh, no, there is nothing wrong. Illya used to talk so much
about his University friends . . . we are expecting another of
Illya's friends to call later this summer, you must know him
. . . Captain Ivan Petrovich Narvinsky.

CHULKATURIN

No, I don't think so.

[ 63 ]

LIZA

Illya used to talk about him all the time. He's the terribly handsome one that I was absolutely forbidden to meet. The one who went into the Army.

CHULKATURIN

No, I'm afraid I don't recall . . .

LIZA

Shall I try to place you? I know all of Illya's friends.

CHULKATURIN

Well, I don't think that outside of being roommates we were very . . .

LIZA

(*Clapping her hands*)

You were the roommate who never came in from parties earlier than four in the morning. The boy who never attended a single lecture for two years.

CHULKATURIN

No. I think that was the roommate your brother had during his senior year. We were roommates during the second year, the first half of the second year. Then Illya moved out.

LIZA

Oh. (*Pause*) Then you must be the one Illya had that terrible fight with over some dreadful woman. He wrote papa all about it in a letter.

[ 64 ]

CHULKATURIN

No. Illya and I never had a quarrel. That was Peter Richter
from Prussia.

LIZA

If you give me time I will remember just exactly your place
in my brother's life, because Illya wrote me without fail a letter
every week from Petersburg and I'm sure I know everything
he did. (*Pause*) You were the one who gambled at the races.
(*A line of pain momentarily crosses* CHULKATURIN'S *face
but the girl does not see it*)

CHULKATURIN

That was Ivan Vorontzoff. I never went to the races.

LIZA

You did not own a white stallion? (CHULKATURIN *shakes his
head*) You know what I think? It will come to me suddenly.
Oh!

CHULKATURIN

What is the matter?

LIZA

I hope you have not come all this way just to see Illya, because he is not here. He left to go abroad for the Czar; he is
in the diplomatic service now you know since last April, but
I'm sure he wrote you about that. (CHULKATURIN *shakes his
head*) No? He must have forgotten. Poor Illya, it was a very
busy time for him so you must excuse him. He left for Austria
a month after his wedding to Frieda Semeonova who is a blood
relative of Prince Adrian. I'm sorry you were unable to come

for the wedding. So many of Illya's friends and yours from the University came, but you must have been busy. (*It is obvious from the look on* CHULKATURIN's *face that he realizes what a small part he must have played in* ILLYA's *life, and that* ILLYA *did not even consider him enough of a friend to extend a wedding invitation to him. He is saved from any further embarrassment by* LIZA *running over to her bullfinch*) Isn't it darling? Illya gave it to me when he left. I have been teaching it to sing. (*To the bird*) Sing a song for the gentleman, Popka. (*She whistles to the bird, then turns to* CHULKATURIN) He really sings his heart out when he wants to. Come. (*Motions for* CHULKATURIN *to come over to the cage. He stands close to* LIZA *as she talks*) See, he is not afraid of you at all. That's a good sign. It is a well-known fact that birds and animals can instinctively look into the hearts of people and know if they are good or bad. Did you know that?

CHULKATURIN

No.

LIZA

Oh, they can. If you trust the judgment of your pets they will always tell you who your real friends are. See how he is not afraid of you.

CHULKATURIN

Then we shall become friends.

LIZA

(*To bird*)

Brave little bird. That's a brave little bird. (*To* CHULKATURIN) I would find it impossible to love someone that an animal feared, wouldn't you?

[ 66 ]

CHULKATURIN

I don't know.

LIZA

Will you whistle for Popka? See if he will sing for you.

CHULKATURIN

Oh, I don't think I could.

LIZA

Please.

(CHULKATURIN, *after a moment's hesitation, begins to whistle*)

ZODITCH

Already he must prove he is an ass. Already the fool.

CHULKATURIN

Is it possible that one day you could open the door to some stranger's house and fall in love? (ZODITCH *lets out a cry of disgust*) Yes, it is possible. That was the exact moment I fell in love. I say that without reservation. The moment the door swung open into that household was the exact moment I came to love and to shut out all the impossible loneliness and misfortune of all the years before: my father's failures, my mother's long-suffering virtues, my less than human isolation from mankind. I had now for the first time placed myself in contact with one whose steps would not flee from me, one whose eyes would behold my face and not turn away. It didn't matter that now I stood in front of a bird's cage and forced myself to whistle. Not even forced myself. I whistled joyfully.

[ 67 ]

ZODITCH

You ass!

CHULKATURIN

The tune, whose melody I can no longer remember, rose
from my heart. A nameless tune from the so long shut closet
of my heart broke forth and I brushed against the sleeve of her
dress and she did not move and the bird broke forth answering
me and I thought as I stood there, God, oh God, don't let me
be shut up any more.

(*Lights out on* CHULKATURIN *scene*)

ZODITCH

What are you talking about? What do you think you're talking about? (*Pours himself a drink. Sound of someone shuffling
about in the hall. The shuffling goes back and forth as* ZODITCH
*drinks.* ZODITCH *goes to the door and listens. In a whispered
voice, as he opens the door a crack*) Who is that?

GREGORY

It's me, Zoditch, Gregory from downstairs.

ZODITCH
(*Practically hissing in annoyance*)

What the devil are you doing marching up and back? Have
you lost your wits?

GREGORY

I must talk to you.

ZODITCH
(*Suspiciously*)

About what?

GREGORY

Let me come in. I don't want to stand in the hallway. (*After some hesitation* ZODITCH *lets him in*)

GREGORY

Something must be done to increase the amount of coal provided the tenants. We will all freeze to death unless steps are taken with Katerina Prolomnaya. The woman is mad to think a family can survive a winter night on half a bucketful of bad coal. Do you know the dogs are freezing to death out on the street? Have you heard even as much as one of them howl tonight? By morning there won't be a live dog left in Petersburg. Already the water basin in my kitchen has pieces of ice in it the size of your fist.

ZODITCH

Why do you bother me with your family problems? Go see Katerina Prolomnaya. I have no time to get involved in this.

GREGORY

That is what must be done. Katerina Prolomnaya must be visited.

ZODITCH

Then go. Go!

GREGORY

That is what my family has instructed me to do. My wife will not put up with it another night. And my children . . . the eyes they turn to me . . . it would break the heart of a monster . . . even Katerina Prolomnaya would see the necessity of more coal if she could hear my children crying in their beds. We must not be ignored because we are poor. She must not be allowed to prey on our misery.

ZODITCH

Then why do you stand here? Be off. Speak to her. This is a family problem.

GREGORY

She must be spoken to. It's not right to be cruel when people are suffering. But I don't know what to say to that woman. Every time I have to speak to her the words tumble together in my mouth. I am no good with words . . . that is why I was in the hall . . . I kept saying if I start down the stairs I will find the right words to make my position clear by the time I reach her door, but then I think what if I knock on her door and she opens it and I do not have the words yet, what then? Eh? What then?

ZODITCH

(Anguished)

What do you want of me? Leave me alone.

GREGORY

And I think what if those rotten brown dogs of hers come for me even while the words are glue in my mouth? How many have those dirty beasts sunk their teeth into already?

ZODITCH

I cannot help this. I want only to be left alone. I am a busy man.

GREGORY

Zoditch, come with me.

[ 70 ]

ZODITCH

What are you saying?

GREGORY

You are a man of words. Everybody knows that. Everybody respects you for that. Just the other day my wife was commenting on your fine methods of address and speech deportment. "How fine Mr. Zoditch speaks. How quickly. How precisely . . . He is a master of the Russian language." You are much in respect because of it. If you went with me the other tenants would follow. I know they would. Come. Come. We will face her together. You will say all the right things. You will say what only you know how to say. One, two, three, it will be done.

ZODITCH

Leave go of my arm. This is not for me. I tell you leave go!
(*Jerks his arm free*)

GREGORY

What are you doing to me? We are neighbors. We live side by side.

ZODITCH

Side by side. Where is that, side by side? When my mother died, who came to me with fruit? When I lay in my bed sick with fever for three days, who knocked on my door? Who said to me, "Zoditch, my friend, we have come. Zoditch, are you alive? Here is soup to warm you, a cool towel for your head. Zoditch, we have come." Nobody. Nobody came.

GREGORY

But nobody knew. Nobody was informed.

[ 71 ]

ZODITCH

(*Pulling open the door*)

Nobody cared! (GREGORY *seems about to say something, then changes his mind. He exits.* ZODITCH *closes the door after him*) Nobody.

(ZODITCH *leans against the door intently listening as* GREGORY *descends the stairs. We hear the shrill barking of a number of small lap dogs.* KATERINA PROLOMNAYA's *door opens and the barking becomes louder and more shrill. Through the barking we hear* GREGORY)

GREGORY

Katerina Prolomnaya, I have come . . . (*The rest is blotted out by the barking. After a moment*) We won't survive the night. Already the frost is through the window. Surely there is enough compassion in you to . . . (*There is the sound, the mad sound, of* KATERINA PROLOMNAYA's *laughter. The barking has increased.* GREGORY *runs up the stairs shouting*) Get them away from me. Get away. You get away. In the name of Christ, if we don't get some more coal . . . Oh God . . . get away . . . aaagh . . . aaagh. Help me. Zoditch, help me. Help me. Get away you bastards. Get away. (*Pounds on* ZODITCH's *door*) Zoditch! Zoditch, help me. Oh God.

(*The scene ends in a wild crescendo of pounding, barking, yelling, and laughter, as* ZODITCH *presses his back to the door*)

ZODITCH

Leave me alone. Leave me alone. This is a family problem!

(*He slides down the door and collapses to the floor*)

CURTAIN

[ 72 ]

# Act Two

PLACE: *The same.* ZODITCH'S *apartment.*
TIME: *A few moments later.*
SCENE: *The same.*
ON RISE: *All sounds have stopped.* GREGORY *is gone.*

ZODITCH

(*Suddenly shouts out, nervously, excitedly, clearly in an anguish of some kind*)

Let the house freeze, Gregory. What else are winters for if not to put frost on dogs! (*Shovels in the remainder of the coal. Stands in front of the stove, his arms wrapped about him*) I am not to freeze. She would be a fool not to take my attainments into consideration. Is it nothing to be a first reader in a famous publishing house? Is it nothing to have read Seneca, Cicero? O tempora! O mores! Senatus haec intellegit, consul videt; hic tamen vivit. Vivit? Where is the wonder then that Katerina Prolomnaya should reach for me? Is it every widow who can snatch twice at the gold ring? (*Goes over to the table and picks up the diary for a second and then puts it down*) Katerina Prolomnaya, do not underestimate my value! I am no ring for your finger without considerations. You are not the voice of springtime. Bear in mind assets. Ah. This marriage is a diminishment for me without your assets. I do not mind the diminishment if there are assets. (*Pulls out a piece of paper and makes notations*) Rents. Movables: tables, chairs, sofas, beds, et cetera. Drapes, linens, clothings, furs, equipments, carriages.

[ 75 ]

Personal assets: the pleasures of the bed . . . marred, gray streaks in the hair, brow wrinkles, crow's-feet, throat wrinkles, worn down teeth, yellow and fallen out teeth, breasts good, too-full waist, a mouth forever at the food box, a brain stuffed with candies. (*Shaking the paper in his hand*) It is well to bear in mind, Katerina, that we do not live by bread alone. In me you will not find a husband who is fondly foolish, one of those husbands who thinks to satisfy a woman's whims is to satisfy all. In me you will have a husband gentle but firm, a husband capable of great understanding and compassion, but a husband capable of being the master of his house, a husband whose hand though not often set down, set down becomes immovable.

(ZODITCH *smashes his hand on the table. And then, satisfied with his speech, picks up the diary.*
*Lights up on* CHULKATURIN)

#### CHULKATURIN

O sweet summer. Sweet lost summer of days that are no more. Summer of bright birds. Summer of flowers. Summer of strawberries and golden mornings. Summer of musical harmonies in the sky. Summer when my heart stood in tune with every living thing. Summer when I was not myself. Summer when I was in love.

(*Lights out on* CHULKATURIN.
*Lights up on a public garden*)

#### KIRILLA
(*Offstage*)

Why don't they watch where they plant their damn vines? Must a man break his skull or strangle to death in order to keep on the path?

BIZMIONKOV

(*Offstage*)

This way, my friend. Be careful. Do not trample down the flowerbeds.

KIRILLA

(*Offstage*)

Is that you, Bizmionkov? Blast their flowerbeds. What idiot planted flowerbeds in a public garden? (*He comes out on stage*) Here, this way. It's clearer over here. (*He plunks down exhausted on the bench.* BIZMIONKOV, *book in hand, calmly appears*) Where's Anna?

BIZMIONKOV

She was with you. You were hand in hand when we left the fountain.

KIRILLA

No. She was with you.

BIZMIONKOV

(*Turns a page*)

I'm sure she was with you.

KIRILLA

Don't be foolish. (*Calls out*) Anna! Anna! (*To* BIZMIONKOV) And where is my daughter? (*Shouts*) Liza! (*To* BIZMIONKOV) This park was designed by a madman whose sole desire is to lose half of Russia in a vine tangle! And where is Chulkaturin? The poor fellow can't find his way from one end of the street to the other.

[ 77 ]

ANNA

*( Halloing from somewhere offstage )*

Yoo hoo. Yoo hoo.

KIRILLA

Anna! Anna! Is that you?

ANNA

*( Offstage )*

Yoo hoo. Yoo hoo.

KIRILLA

Over here, woman. Yoo hoo. Yoo hoo.

ANNA

*( Offstage )*

I can't.

KIRILLA

What do you mean you can't?

ANNA

*( Offstage )*

I'm in the middle of a flowerbed.

BIZMIONKOV

Watch how you step, Anna. Don't crush the flowers.

KIRILLA

*( To* BIZMIONKOV ) The devil take the flowers.

*( To* ANNA ) Come forward. Watch the vines; damn the flowers!

*( Sound of* ANNA *crashing through the brush )*

[ 78 ]

ANNA
(*Offstage*)
I'm coming. I'm coming. Yoo hoo. Yoo hoo.

KIRILLA
I can assure you, my friend, this park will be looked into. Monstrosities do not just create themselves. There are madmen at work here. (ANNA *breaks into the clearing. Her large white hat is crushed*) You see? You see? Look what those madmen have done to my wife.

BIZMIONKOV
It is only a matter of staying on the path, my dear friend. It is all geometrically laid out. One has only to follow the path.

KIRILLA
Bah! Here, Anna, sit on the bench. (*To* BIZMIONKOV) We will see what is geometrically laid out and what is not. Do they imagine we are bees? My poor Anna.

ANNA
(*Practically in tears*)
Oh, my hat.

BIZMIONKOV
They do not imagine we are bees.

KIRILLA
They think because we are an outlying province they can send their madmen out here to create monstrosities, but that is a mistake, I can assure you. The businessmen of this town will not put up with it.

[ 79 ]

ANNA

Oh, my hat.


KIRILLA

(*In a quick aside to his wife*)

Enough with the hat, Anna. (*To* BIZMIONKOV) I have a son in the diplomatic service. All I have to do is write a letter and there will be repercussions. It isn't every family that has a son involved in the intricate workings of government, or is expecting a visit from a captain of cavalry.


BIZMIONKOV

The diplomatic service and the park department are totally separate.


KIRILLA

Ah, you think so. But you are mistaken. They are hand in glove.


ANNA

My hat, look at what has happened to my hat.


KIRILLA

Enough with the hat! (*To* BIZMIONKOV) It is only to a political novice such as yourself, Bizmionkov, that things appear unrelated. In government the toe is connected to the foot and the foot to the arm and so forth.


BIZMIONKOV

The Department of Parks is connected to the Department of Fish. It is not connected to diplomatic service.

[ 80 ]

### KIRILLA

(*Calls, after giving* BIZMIONKOV *an angry stare*)

Liza! (*To* BIZMIONKOV) That is only what they want you to think, Bizmionkov. Listen to me. I am aware of what is and what is not.

### ANNA

And where is Elizaveta? You were holding her hand when we left the fountain.

### KIRILLA

I was not holding her hand when we left the fountain. Do not exasperate me, Anna. (*Shouts*) Liza! (*To* BIZMIONKOV) There are things I could tell you about the working of the government that would completely shock you. You would say to me, "Kirilla Matveich, that is impossible. Kirilla Matveich, you are mad, such things cannot be."

### ANNA

She is lost.

### KIRILLA

She is not lost. She is with Chulkaturin.

### KIRILLA and ANNA

(*Suddenly aware that to be with* CHULKATURIN *is to be lost, both call out*)

Liza! Liza! (*They exit.* BIZMIONKOV *follows, reading his book.*

*Sound of* LIZA's *laughter is heard.* LIZA *bursts out into the open and whirls herself around.* CHULKATURIN *appears and watches her as she is lost in her reveries. She spirals to*

[ 81 ]

*the ground. For a long moment she remains on the floor*
*of the forest as* CHULKATURIN *stares at her* )

ZODITCH

Go to the Petersburg ballet! Don't dance on my time! This
is not the ballet!

CHULKATURIN

I could not move. I could not breathe. There were wildflowers in her hand. Her cheek pressed to the floor of the
forest as if feeling the unheard music of grass and earth. I
clung to the edge of the clearing afraid to approach, afraid to
be seen, afraid of a moment into which I had transgressed.
Though love had brought me, I came only as a stranger.

(LIZA, *resting on her extended arm, slowly opens her*
*eyes and stares at* CHULKATURIN. *The moment is poignant*
*and* CHULKATURIN *breaks the mood abruptly by striding*
*forward in cheerful embarrassment* )

CHULKATURIN

( *A bit too loud* )

Well, you see you have fallen. That's what you get for running so fast. Come. Let me help you up.

( *Extends his hand to her. She looks at him for a moment*
*and then turns away. He drops his hand* )

LIZA

I'm all right. Please, just a moment.

CHULKATURIN

( *Stands by her, uneasily feeling that something should*
*be said but not knowing, or rather not daring, to say what*
*is in his heart. Instead, he makes conversation* )

I suppose they will be wondering what happened to us. I cannot imagine how we came to be separated from your parents. (*Pause in which there is no answer*) Well, we've certainly taken our exercise for the day. If the summer continues at such a pace we shall all be in fine health. I haven't run this far since my father raced me in the meadows of Lambswater. (*Pause. Change of tone. Serious*) You grow older you run less.

LIZA

(*Suddenly turning to him*)
You think it was childish of me to run?

CHULKATURIN
No. No, I didn't mean to imply that.

LIZA
Well, it was. Perhaps it will be a long time before I run again. (*Her mood changes from seriousness to fresh exuberance*) Come. Sit down beside me.
(*Extending her hand to him as he had before to her*)

CHULKATURIN
We ought to sit on the bench. Your dress is going to be covered with grass stains.

LIZA
(*She drops her hand as he, before, had dropped his. She becomes thoughtful for a second and then that passes and she smiles again, playfully*)
If you make me sit on the bench, I shall fold my hands in my lap and not allow you to become what you should become.

[ 83 ]

CHULKATURIN

And what is that?

LIZA

What do you think that is?

CHULKATURIN

I don't know.

LIZA

Guess.

CHULKATURIN

I can't.

LIZA

Then you shan't become it.
                    (*She plays with the wildflowers*)

CHULKATURIN

Tell me.

LIZA

What would you like to become?

CHULKATURIN

I don't know.

LIZA

Poor Nikolai Alexeevich Chulkaturin doesn't know what he would like to become. Shall I be kind and tell you, then?

[ 84 ]

(*Pause, and she breaks into a smile*) King of the May! The king of all the hearts of young ladies. Here and now I shall give you your new identity. But you must kneel properly and lower your head. Come. On your knees, or else I shall be forced to find another to be King of the May and you shall have lost your identity for good. Don't dally. Shall you be crowned or not? (*There is a moment in which they look at each other directly in the eyes, and then* CHULKATURIN *goes on his knees and lowers his head. She begins putting the wildflowers in his hair*) What fine silky hair you have, Nikolai Alexeevich. Have there been many young ladies who have loved you for your fine brown hair?

CHULKATURIN

There has been no one.

LIZA

Perhaps you have forgotten them. The woods are full of the sighs of young girls. I think there must be many girls you have loved and forgotten.

CHULKATURIN

Do not think that there have been others.

LIZA

You must hold still. If you raise your head the flowers will fall.

CHULKATURIN

There has been no one who has loved me. Do not think that of me.

[ 85 ]

LIZA

I think men must be very cruel creatures to play with the heart of a girl and then not even remember her name. Men are like that according to my brother.

(*She laughs*)

CHULKATURIN

Why do you laugh?

LIZA

Illya says that the hearts of young girls are strewn about the world like grains of sand upon the shore and that there are not as many stars in the night sky as unremembered girls. Do you think that is true?

CHULKATURIN

I think that is poetic.

LIZA

And is that the same as true? What is your answer to that, Nikolai Alexeevich who has fine silky hair?

CHULKATURIN

You are making fun of me.

LIZA

(*Stops as if suddenly wearied*)

Yes.

(*She stands up and turns to face the sun*)

CHULKATURIN

Have I offended you?

[ 86 ]

LIZA
*(Wearily)*

No.

CHULKATURIN

Then what is the matter? Why are you staring into the sun?

LIZA

Must I have reasons for everything? Is it not enough reason to stare at the sun because it is up there, because it is flaming across the sky, because we may never see the light again, because, because, because, because. (*The mood becomes a trifle lighter as if she attempted to recover*) Have I found enough "becauses" to satisfy you? (*He is hurt. She reaches out to him, sincerely*) Poor Nikolai, it is I who have offended you. Am I completely intolerable to be with?

CHULKATURIN
*(As he stands up, the flowers fall off his head)*

No. You cannot offend me. How could you ever think that you . . .

LIZA

See how soon every flower must fall. (*Brushing her hand through his hair to dislodge the other flowers*) Every flower. (*To* CHULKATURIN) Don't be angry with me, ever, Nikolai. (*She takes his hands in hers and kisses them.* CHULKATURIN *bends down to kiss her, but she almost flippantly turns away*) Papa thinks young girls should be placed in hibernation along with Siberian Mastodons until we become eighteen years old, then we are to be melted from the ice and returned to our homes in time for marriage. Isn't that terribly clever of papa?
*(She begins to cry)*

CHULKATURIN

(*In surprise and confusion*)

Liza, why are you crying?

LIZA

(*Tears running*)

Isn't that terribly clever. I suppose I should take my dear bullfinch to sing to me in the ice and . . .

CHULKATURIN

What is wrong? Please don't cry. Please, Liza, Liza. Please! (*She turns her back to* CHULKATURIN *and, bowing her head, runs off.* CHULKATURIN *picks up the fallen flowers*) Are the tears of women ever insignificant? And the tears of young girls, the young girls of our youth that so haunt us in after years, are they so much salt water lost from us forever? Did she not then standing there in the final light of the sun, love me? Think, think, if I could not claim every tear, might not there have been a single tear that was for me, a fragment of a tear, a thousandth part of all that running flood loosed for me? For me alone? Could those tears have fallen without me?

ZODITCH

They fall. They fall. Having no mind of their own, women have tears. It is not necessary to philosophize these things.

CHULKATURIN

I danced that night. I opened every window to the summer air, struck every candle, from every corner of the room dispelled every shadow. I took the wine from the landlord's table and brought it to my room. I took the books from the shelves

and threw them in the closet. I locked the closet. The tears of
a young girl, no . . . the tears of a young woman are bashful
trembling tears. Shall I quote to you important works of important philosophers that will tell you that, precisely just that?
There is no other way for girls to come to love but through
tears. Shall I tell you about my future plans? In my happiness,
my love, I made future plans. The world was to become involved with me, and I, through Liza, like some rose flung to
the shores of the universe was to become involved with the
world. There was the plan involving a wedding that the little
provincial town would never forget. The entire town was to
be invited, down to the last shoemaker.

ZODITCH

You cannot make weddings out of tears! There is nothing
written down here to make weddings from! What are you making weddings from?
(*Furiously begins re-reading the previous pages. He
turns the pages backward and forward while* CHULKATURIN
*goes on in his happiness*)

CHULKATURIN

Why should not the lowest shoemaker share in my happiness? I wanted everybody that I had ever brushed against to
be happy. Let all those whose hearts were sick, be healed. Let
those who were pained in silence, be pained no more. I saw
the house of the Ozhogins preparing for the feast. Tables
decked out: linen cloths, silverware, breads, steaming urns of
soup, caviar, chicken boiled, chicken roasted, assortments of
dainties, teas black and green, chocolates and mints, fruits,
oranges, lots of oranges.

[ 89 ]

ZODITCH

(*Calling out while hunting for anything written that might have provoked* CHULKATURIN's *outburst*)

Insane madman! You are making a wedding out of nothing!

CHULKATURIN

Old man Ozhogin stuffed into his leather chair, delightful, wondrous old man Ozhogin, patting his stuffed belly, checking the time with a gold watch drawn from his vest, blowing fantastic vast clouds of tobacco from a miraculous black cigar; my father's watch, I had given Father Ozhogin my father's watch, and Mother Ozhogin crying tears on her voluminous breasts, she was my mother now . . . (ZODITCH *lets out a cry of disgust*) I had a family . . . Ozhogin . . . how rich that simple name sounded . . . Ozhogin . . . has there ever been a more lovely name? A more beautiful sound upon the air? And Liza, my Liza before me in her wedding dress, her long unbound hair fallen to her shoulders, her eyes lit with happiness. The happiness that would be mine forever.

(*Lights out on* CHULKATURIN)

ZODITCH

No more of this!

(*Starts flipping the pages for a new beginning. As he hunts, a spotlight falls on* CAPTAIN IVAN PETROVICH NARVINSKY, *a spit and polish officer. The kind of young man that traditionally sways a young girl's heart . . . he is* RUBIN. *The captain is apparently engaged in conversation with others.*

*Spotlight on* CHULKATURIN)

[ 90 ]

CHULKATURIN

In brass, in leather, in saddle soap, the captain of cavalry called. Volobrina. (VOLOBRINA *approaches . . . She is* FEATHERS) Who is that?

VOLOBRINA

The friend of Illya's, Ivan Petrovitch. A distinguished officer and rich. Come to organize recruits for the Czar.

CHULKATURIN

Illya's friend, ah. What the hell does he want here? Doesn't he know Illya isn't at home?

VOLOBRINA

What does anyone want here? Eh? (*She goes.*
    *Lights go up on the* OZHOGIN *living room. Present are the* CAPTAIN, KIRILLA, ANNA, BIZMIONKOV *and* LIZA)

CAPTAIN

At present my stay in this district is quite indefinite. A month, perhaps two. It is difficult to say at the outset.

ANNA

And have you found a suitable place to stay, Ivan Petrovich?

CAPTAIN

Yes, thank you. I have engaged a number of rooms at the inn for my officers and myself.

BIZMIONKOV

I'm afraid you will find the inn somewhat less than what you are accustomed to.

KIRILLA

I'm sure that will be the case. There are no decent accommodations in this entire town.

BIZMIONKOV

But then hardly anyone ever comes here, so there never seems any pressing need to have decent accommodations.
(ANNA *laughs at the little joke*)

CAPTAIN

I am a soldier, Mr. Bizmionkov, and for a soldier luxury is an unnecessary vice.

BIZMIONKOV

Yes, of course.

CAPTAIN

A soldier must take the terrain as he finds it. If he finds his feet are wet, well, then he must accept his wet feet. In my life such things are of no significance.

BIZMIONKOV

And what is of significance, Ivan Petrovich?

CAPTAIN

To serve the Czar and the motherland. To fight the enemies of Russia and to serve with courage and with faith.

LIZA
(*With a sigh*)

Yes, that is right.
(*Before she has a chance to be embarrassed at her outburst,* CHULKATURIN *enters the room waving a white rose*)

[ 92 ]

CHULKATURIN

Good day. Good day. (*They all turn toward* CHULKATURIN. *The* CAPTAIN *alone stands*) Oh, you have a guest! (*As if in complete surprise*) I hope I'm not intruding, but I was just passing by and . . . (*In his gesture, the rose flies out of his grasp and lands at* LIZA's *foot. He tries to remain nonchalant*) Oh. (*He hastens to get it*) I thought since I was in the vicinity I would come over. (LIZA *hands him the flower. They briefly exchange glances. He doesn't know quite what to do with the rose. It occupies much of his attention*) I hope I'm not intruding.

KIRILLA

(*With a trace of irritation in his voice*)
Not a bit.

CHULKATURIN

Are you sure?

KIRILLA

Yes. Yes. Quite all right.

CHULKATURIN

Because if you wish I could return later. I do not wish to interrupt.

(*Looking about him for a friendly smile*)

KIRILLA

(*Impatiently*)
You are not interrupting! May I present Captain Ivan Petrovich Narvinsky, an officer in the Czar's cavalry. Captain, this is Nikolai Alexeevich Chulka . . .

[ 93 ]

CHULKATURIN

(*Used to his name being mishandled, completes it*)
Chulkaturin.

KIRILLA

Chulkaturin. A friend of Illya's from the University.

CAPTAIN

Ah! A pleasure, sir.
    (CHULKATURIN *has started to shake hands. However, all
the* CAPTAIN *intended to do was a slight click of the heels
and a bow. When he sees* CHULKATURIN *intends to shake
hands, he extends his hand.* CHULKATURIN, *unfortunately,
raises the hand with the rose. He switches the rose to the
other hand. They finally shake*)

CHULKATURIN

Thank you. Thank you. A pleasure for me as well. (*A kind
of silence settles on the room*) Well, please go on with whatever you were discussing. I'll just sit here.
    (*Starts to sit on the step leading into the living room.
A step near* LIZA)

CAPTAIN

No, please.
                (*Offers* CHULKATURIN *his chair*)

CHULKATURIN

Oh no. Please. It's quite all right here. I really don't mind in
the least.

KIRILLA

What? Is that our last chair? I have a thousand chairs in this house. Wait.

(*Starts to head out of the living room*)

CHULKATURIN

Please. There is no need to bother. I'm perfectly . . .

KIRILLA

There is a need. Nobody has to sit on floors in my living room.

(*Glares at* CHULKATURIN *and marches out. Silence descends. Finally . . .*)

CAPTAIN

So you knew Illya from the University, Mr. Chulkaturin.

CHULKATURIN

Yes, from the University.

CAPTAIN

Ah!

(*Followed by a pause. A noticeable lapse in the conversation*)

CHULKATURIN
(*Starts the conversation again*)
Is that where you knew Illya from?

CAPTAIN

Yes.

CHULKATURIN

Ah!

(*Another noticeable pause*)

CAPTAIN

Perhaps we've met before?

CHULKATURIN

I don't think so.

CAPTAIN

Ah. (*Pause*) Were you one of the gentlemen Illya brought to my father's summer home?

CHULKATURIN

No.

CAPTAIN

It was a hunting trip?

CHULKATURIN

I don't hunt.

CAPTAIN

Oh.

(*Pause*)

ANNA

The captain is here to recruit soldiers for the Czar's cavalry.

CHULKATURIN

So?

CAPTAIN

Yes.

(*Pause*)

BIZMIONKOV
(*Opening his watch*)

Almost noon.

(*Snaps his watch shut. Sound of chair scraping in the hall. Some grunting on the part of* KIRILLA)

CHULKATURIN

Let me help, Mr. Ozhogin. I'll give you a hand.
(*Goes offstage.*
*We hear them speak*)

KIRILLA
(*Offstage*)

No. It's all right.

CHULKATURIN
(*Offstage*)

I'll take the leg.

KIRILLA
(*Offstage*)

I have it by myself. Watch your flower. You're pushing the flower in my eye. Watch it! Watch it!
(*Sound of the chair falling over*)

ANNA
(*Rising*)

What's happened?

CHULKATURIN

(*Pokes his head in. The flower is bent*)

We've got it now.

KIRILLA

(*Appears holding the chair by himself.* CHULKATURIN *uselessly hovers about him*)

I can manage by myself.

ANNA

Are you all right?

KIRILLA

(*Sets the chair down*)

Fine. Just fine. (*To* CHULKATURIN) Sit!

(CHULKATURIN *sits.* KIRILLA *returns to his seat. He blinks his eye*)

LIZA

Is your eye all right, papa?

KIRILLA

Yes. Yes. Go on with your conversation.

(*Pause. Silence.* BIZMIONKOV *coughs. More silence*)

CHULKATURIN

Would you like to take a turn around the garden, Mrs. Ozhogin? Liza?

ANNA

Perhaps after a bit, thank you.

(LIZA *just shakes her head.* BIZMIONKOV *coughs again*)

CHULKATURIN

Allow me to get you some water.

BIZMIONKOV

No need . . . Just a tickle.

CHULKATURIN

Quite all right. I'll be back in a moment.
(*Gets up and heads for kitchen. Conversation immediately picks up*)

KIRILLA

You were saying, my dear captain?

LIZA

Ivan Petrovich was telling us about the cruel conditions under which soldiers must live, papa.
(*Lights dim on scene in living room. The rest of their conversation is played out in mime. Light focuses gradually down on the* CAPTAIN, *who continues speaking, and* LIZA, *who becomes more and more absorbed.* CHULKATURIN *has returned. He stands spotlighted in the doorway, a rose in one hand, a glass of water in the other*)

CHULKATURIN

So he talked and so she listened and so you see . . . you see what it is to exist as an interruption, a break in everybody's conversation.

ZODITCH

(*Shouting out*)

Nobody is just a break in the conversation! We all have our place! From the peasant to the Czar we have our place. Every

[ 99 ]

ant, every roach has his place. This is God's universe. This is not a madhouse of useless, placeless rats.

CHULKATURIN

How well the conversation proceeds now that I have left. Bizmionkov no longer coughs. He no longer even finds it necessary to clear his throat. Papa Ozhogin is no longer set to the task of moving chairs; Mama Ozhogin does not have to refuse a walk in the garden. Everybody is dug in. Conversation, now that I am gone, becomes pure song. (CHULKATURIN *extends his hand holding the rose*) For you, Liza. Did you not know the rose was for you? Do young men carry roses for nothing? (*Only* LIZA *and* CAPTAIN *are now visible in living room*) Go on, you Othello of the Steppes, with your big wars, your killings, your medals. Go on, Liza, fall in love with his black boots, his moustache, his eyes, and gallantries. What could I bring to you to match those gifts? And you, stand in the arches of the doorway with your water glass and your rose, stand there until the sky falls down, for all the difference it makes. It should have been enough for you to sleep through life, dreaming of happiness. (*Light goes out on* LIZA *and* CAPTAIN) Oh time that was and time that never more shall be, I give you back your woods, your pathways, your shadowed glades. I give you back her whose dear sweet lips once brushed my heart. I give you back the earth I knelt upon to take a crown. I give you back the happiness of days now fled from me. I give back . . . I . . . (*Sound of waltz music growing louder*) No. No. Nothing! I give back nothing! (*A lighted chandelier is lowered from the ceiling onto the center of the stage. Bit by bit, as* CHULKATURIN *stares about him, a dance is assembled. A table of punch, fruit, cookies, is brought in by a number of the* CAPTAIN's *officers. We*

*hear the chatter of people, the music, the laughter. In the wings
of the stage, left and right, we can see some of the dancers. A
young woman, perhaps twenty-five years of age, enters the
stage behind* CHULKATURIN. *She pauses momentarily at the
punch bowl and then, eyeing* CHULKATURIN, *comes forward. On
her head quivers a small butterfly attached to a copper spring.
The girl has an awkward smile that is constantly being flashed.
She is the girl left over, the girl unchosen by any man.* CHULKA-
TURIN, *in his anguish, cries out to the world and to the vanished*
LIZA) Nothing was definite until the night of the dance. Listen,
I am not the type that deludes himself. You were no more his
than mine the night of the dance. No more mine . . . (*Voice
trails off as if suddenly awake he is now at the dance*) than his.
Why do you play games with me?

TANIA

(*Flirting as best as she can. She occasionally strikes*
CHULKATURIN *with her fan*)
I still think it's mighty strange, Mr. Chulkaturin, that you
could be in our little town so many months and we never meeting. I bet you just came in for the dance.

CHULKATURIN

(*Scarcely hears her, he is so distraught*)
What?

TANIA

I said isn't it strange we never met previously. I just bet you
came in for the dance. Everybody does.

CHULKATURIN

Came in where?

[ 101 ]

TANIA

Why, in town.

CHULKATURIN

No. No. I've been here for months.

TANIA

Isn't it strange we've never met before?

CHULKATURIN

Yes. Strange, very strange.

TANIA

Just everybody is here tonight. Just everybody. I think someone has done something to the punch. Everybody seems to be
having such a gay time, don't you think? I just love dances. I
can't seem to remember who I am when I'm dancing. Isn't that
funny? I start out saying, "Tania, you must remember your own
name, you silly girl, you mustn't forget your own name," but
then I feel myself saying "one, two, three, one, two, three," and
the room begins spinning around and around, and the music
seems to slide right into my slippers. (*There is no response
from* CHULKATURIN. *She waves to someone*) So many of the
gentlemen I know seem to be absent tonight.

(LIZA *and the* CAPTAIN *waltz by, from wing to wing of
the stage, totally ignoring* CHULKATURIN)

CHULKATURIN

Did he say something to me? Did you hear him say something to me when he danced by?

TANIA

The Captain?

[ 102 ]

CHULKATURIN

Yes. Yes. Him.

TANIA

Why I'm sure I don't know. I don't think so, Mr. Chulkaturin.
Isn't he a handsome man in that lovely uniform.

CHULKATURIN

He made a noise.

TANIA

Is something wrong, Mr. Chulkaturin?

CHULKATURIN

No. Why should there be something wrong?

TANIA

I don't know.

CHULKATURIN

That what are you talking about? Let's dance. (CHULKATURIN
*dances wildly, angrily. He begins to shout as he dances. The
girl becomes increasingly distressed. On one of the turns, he
half thrusts her from him. He continues shouting as he dances
alone.* TANIA, *frightened, watches him for a moment and runs
from the room*) You provincials. You eaters of onions. You
sleepers with sheep. Who invited you to the dance? Who told
you to come? Wasn't it enough you had your fat-legged wives?
Your pimple-nosed children? And you, Captain of Killing,
weren't there enough women in Petersburg to satisfy you? Let
me tell you my friend — go polish your boots in another neigh-

borhood. Why didn't you stay away from what's mine? Did I come around bothering your women? Did I ever come to Petersburg and bother your women? Did I ever take what was yours?

(*The* CAPTAIN *enters in time to hear* CHULKATURIN's *last few words and to see the girl flee.* CHULKATURIN *does not see him. The* CAPTAIN *pretends he has seen nothing. He heads toward the punch bowl*)

CAPTAIN

Ah, Mr. Chulkaturin. Where have you been keeping yourself all evening? Are you enjoying yourself?

CHULKATURIN

Do not mock me!

CAPTAIN

What?

CHULKATURIN

It is you who deserves to be mocked, you hollow-brained imitation of a peacock.

CAPTAIN

(*Holding the glasses full of punch*)

In a moment.

CHULKATURIN

I'll kick your head in if you laugh at me.

CAPTAIN

(*Smiling*)

Not here. In a moment. I understand you.

CHULKATURIN

(*Whispering furiously as he departs*)
Go back to Petersburg.

(*The* CAPTAIN *gives the drink to* VOLOBRINA, *who is passing by with a serving tray. He returns*)

CAPTAIN

(*Smiling. Puts his arm around* CHULKATURIN)
I believe we have some business to discuss.

CHULKATURIN

Take your hands off me. I am not one of your serfs.

CAPTAIN

Keep your voice down. There is no need not to handle this as gentlemen. I assume I am talking to a gentleman.

(*Waves at* LIZA *as she passes by arm in arm with* BIZ-MIONKOV)

CHULKATURIN

Assume what you like.

CAPTAIN

I believe you have intentionally insulted me.

CHULKATURIN

Believe what you like.

CAPTAIN

Perhaps you would prefer to settle this in a duel?

CHULKATURIN

As you wish.

CAPTAIN

If you do not withdraw your remarks it shall be my wish to challenge you. It will also be my unfortunate choice to have to kill you. Let me assure you I am an excellent shot. Therefore, consider what you are forcing me into. I do not wish to kill a man who means nothing to me one way or the other.

CHULKATURIN

Nothing, is it? I withdraw nothing, you fop, you strutting suit of peacock feathers. You think because I am not a soldier I do not know the meaning of courage? You think because I do not have brass bands and medals I do not know how to behave when I am mocked?

CAPTAIN

You mock yourself, sir. But as you wish. I shall have the honor of sending my second to you tomorrow morning, Mr. Stuccoturin.

(CAPTAIN *turns and walks away, smiling, greeting others*)

CHULKATURIN

Chulkaturin! My name is Chulkaturin!

(*A circle of light illuminates* BIZMIONKOV *and* CHULKA-TURIN. *Light on dance scene dims*)

BIZMIONKOV

Listen to me, Chulkaturin, you cannot persist in this. Do you hear his officers? They are laughing because they think you are a fool. They know he will kill you.

[ 106 ]

CHULKATURIN

That is their prerogative. Perhaps tomorrow I shall give them less cause for laughter than they think.

BIZMIONKOV

Have you ever fired a pistol?

CHULKATURIN

No.

BIZMIONKOV

Then you are a fool. He will kill you. He will not miss.

CHULKATURIN

Perhaps.

BIZMIONKOV

Not perhaps, certainly! Do you wish to die? Is that it?

CHULKATURIN

I do not wish to die.

BIZMIONKOV

Do not be too sure of that, my young friend. Many a man has died thinking he did not wish to die.

CHULKATURIN

If you think that you do not understand the meaning of honor.

BIZMIONKOV

This is not a question of honor.

[ 107 ]

CHULKATURIN

He has insulted me. Something was said.

BIZMIONKOV

What was said? (*Long pause in which no answer comes from* CHULKATURIN) What? Are your sensibilities so refined you cannot even say what has been this insult to your honor? Listen to me, go away, tonight. There is nothing for you here. You cannot make a woman love you. Not if you stood on your head till kingdom come. If you can learn that by the time you are twenty-five, you have learned much.

CHULKATURIN

You do not understand.

BIZMIONKOV

Then tell me. Tell me what it is I am to understand. Because I am glad it is not for love that you are putting your back to the wall. Because I am very glad you are not dying for love, because at this very moment the captain's affair is progressing in the back of the Ozhogin garden, in a closed carriage, in the captain's bedroom, or wherever else they have found convenient.

CHULKATURIN

Why do you lie to me?

BIZMIONKOV

Go home, my friend, go home. Do not die uselessly.
(BIZMIONKOV *starts to exit*)

[ 108 ]

CHULKATURIN

(*Shouting after him, and as* CHULKATURIN *turns toward*
BIZMIONKOV *a light goes on showing the* CAPTAIN *kissing*
LIZA)

It is not useless! Don't tell me what is useless! I at least am
not a sponge. I do not hang onto the coattails of a family and
rob them of their food because they have money! I do not pretend friendship where there is none.

ZODITCH

(*Shouts out*)

Go on! Give it to her! Press her into the wall, Rubin! (*The
scene fades out*) Why don't you write about that? That's what
the public wants to read about. There's a man to handle every
bitch . . . And they're all bitches. They take your heart. They
. . . they . . .

(*The scene lights up and we are on the dueling field. On
one side of the stage stands* CHULKATURIN *and on the other
side the* CAPTAIN *and some of his officers. One of the officers,* LIEUTENANT ZIMIN, *slightly drunk, comes over*)

LIEUTENANT ZIMIN

Listen, Tulkaturbin or whatever the hell your name is, can
you handle a military pistol?

CHULKATURIN

Yes.

LIEUTENANT ZIMIN

(*Looks at* CHULKATURIN *dubiously for a second and then
shouts out to the other officers*)

[ 109 ]

You better watch out, Ivan Petrovich. He says he's fired a pistol before. (*The other officers laugh.* ZIMIN *and the* CAPTAIN *do not. The* CAPTAIN *hushes the others. To* CHULKATURIN) All right, Tulkaturbin, I'm going to give you some advice. The captain has no desire to blow your head off. Until you insulted him he didn't even know you existed. Take my advice, apologize and the affair is ended. (*Belches*) Pardon. Then we can all go back to the inn and go to sleep. It's too early in the day for you to die. You're a bright fellow. What lies between the hammer and the anvil soon gets knocked flat. Huh? You understand me? Why get your nose knocked out of joint by interfering in a love affair? Go down to the stage line. Every coach brings in a new woman.

OFFICER A
(*From one of the group by the* CAPTAIN)
Lieutenant Zimin, are you ready?

LIEUTENANT ZIMIN
(*Looks at* CHULKATURIN, *who remains impassive*)
My friend, it is imbeciles such as yourself who ruin the summer. (*To* OFFICER A) We are ready. (*To* CHULKATURIN) There is one round in the pistol so you will have only one opportunity to fire. You understand?

CHULKATURIN
Yes.

LIEUTENANT ZIMIN
When he tells you to cock your pistol you pull this back with your thumb. (*Indicates the hammer.* ZIMIN *pulls back the hammer, and then releases it to show* CHULKATURIN *how it's done*)

[ 110 ]

You see? Don't be too much in a rush to fire. There are no prizes for firing first. (CHULKATURIN *nods*) All right. Let's go. Take off your coat. Give it to me.

(CHULKATURIN *and* ZIMIN *walk to meet the* CAPTAIN's *party in the middle of the stage*)

OFFICER A

Take your positions.

LIEUTENANT ZIMIN

(*To* CHULKATURIN, *who doesn't quite know what to do*) Here, turn around.

(*He turns* CHULKATURIN *around so* CHULKATURIN *and the* CAPTAIN *are back to back*)

OFFICER A

Are you both ready?

CAPTAIN

Yes.

CHULKATURIN

Yes.

OFFICER A

You will each take five paces. At the command, "Turn," you will turn and fire.

OFFICER B

(*One of the ones who has been laughing*)
Has anyone found out where we're supposed to ship the poor fellow's body?

[ 111 ]

CAPTAIN

(*Turning on him*)

Be still!

OFFICER A

Cock your pistols.

(CHULKATURIN's *hand is shaking slightly. He has trouble cocking his pistol.* ZIMIN *cocks it for him*)

Take your paces.

(ZIMIN, OFFICER A, *and the rest back away from the line of fire as the paces are counted off. The* CAPTAIN *and* CHULKATURIN *have come to a stop*)

OFFICER A

Turn! (CHULKATURIN *turns quickly and fires. The* CAPTAIN *is grazed along the temple. He goes down for a moment.* CHULKATURIN *instinctively moves forward*) Stand your place, sir.

(CHULKATURIN *stands still. Head erect, the pistol hanging in his limp arm, he is obviously willing to die. The* CAPTAIN *returns to a standing position and after a moment's hesitation, at which time his pistol is leveled straight at* CHULKATURIN's *head, fires into the air.* CHULKATURIN *gives a long scream of anguish*)

CHULKATURIN

Shoot me! Shoot me! Shoot! Shoot! (*Lights out. We hear the sound of scuffling.* CHULKATURIN *calls out from the dark*)

Where's he going? Take your hands off me. Leave me alone. Come back! Shoot! Shoot me!

(*Lights up on* CHULKATURIN *in his bedroom. He is writhing on the floor, the* DOCTOR *and* TERENTIEVNA *trying to hold him down. It is a melee with his last amount of energy. He*

[ 112 ]

*appears hysterical. He seems to be wanting to pull himself
out of the* DOCTOR's *grasp to get at the* CAPTAIN *in the scene
before*)

DOCTOR

There's nobody. Nobody wants to shoot you.

CHULKATURIN

(*To* DOCTOR)

Listen, you don't know what that little scar across his temple
did to me. Nobody in town spoke to me again. They didn't let
me come to their doors because I who wasn't worth the killing
had tried to kill the captain. She wouldn't see me. What right
did he have to fire into the air? What right did he have to scorn
me so? What right to injure me twice?

DOCTOR

Help me get him to lie down, Terentievna.

CHULKATURIN

Did I deserve that treatment? What right did he have to
shoot into the air? What was I supposed to do? Take his insults
lying down? Don't snakes bite the foot that crushes them?
Even snakes. Just because I'm superfluous, am I to be stepped
on?

(*They get him into the bed*)

DOCTOR

Where was he going? Why is he dressed, Terentievna?

TERENTIEVNA

I don't know, sir. He said he was going to a dance.

[ 113 ]

DOCTOR

Take off his boots. What nonsense!
(*She begins pulling off his boots*)

CHULKATURIN

And who was right, after all? After they didn't speak to me,
after all the doors shut, after I wandered the streets like a
ghost for weeks, when they came around to me. So who was
right, after all? "Chulkaturin," and they knew my name, "you
were right. Listen, my friend, he has made her pregnant and
has deserted her. He has gone back to Petersburg. He has
moved out with his recruits. What is to be done? Who will
marry her now?" (CHULKATURIN *looks hard at the* DOCTOR *and*
TERENTIEVNA. *They both stare at him*) Eh? Who will marry
her? You know how it is with those springtime fellows? Eh?
One flower in April, one flower in May. His day, his hour, was
my whole summer, my whole life.
(CHULKATURIN *stares off in the distance and a spotlight*
*illuminates* KIRILLA *and* ANNA, *who seem to be addressing*
CHULKATURIN)

KIRILLA

Chulkaturin, how clever you are. You knew what that fellow
was from the start. You saw through him, my friend, when the
rest of us were blind. My friend, what are words? What can I
say?

ANNA

She goes nowhere now. She will not leave the house. She is
invited nowhere. What can I say to you?
(*Lights out on* KIRILLA *and* ANNA)

[ 114 ]

DOCTOR
(*To* TERENTIEVNA)
Get me the pan. We must remove the excess blood before it
is too late. (*She exits. To* CHULKATURIN) Be calm, my friend,
be calm. What are you staring at?


CHULKATURIN
What if I gave myself to her now? What if I offered to marry
her? You understand how it was? She was proved worthless,
dishonored. It would be a sacrifice for me to go to her and
propose marriage. It would be an act of pity to love what others
mocked. She would fall into my arms. She would bless me. She
would think I was her savior. That was a proper expectation.
A reasonable man would call it a proper expectation.


DOCTOR
Yes. Yes.


CHULKATURIN
Listen, they've taken my father's boots. Find out what they've
done with my father's boots.


DOCTOR
Don't worry about the boots now.


CHULKATURIN
(*Tears running down his face*)
Don't let them steal the boots. Can I rely on you? Don't let
them steal my property. See to it. See to it. I rely on you.
(*Lights out on scene. Lights full up on* ZODITCH *at his
desk, the diary open,* FEATHERS *standing by his side*)

[ 115 ]

ZODITCH

Well? Well? Was that all?

FEATHERS

Katerina Prolomnaya says that if you wish to come down then you are free to come down, Mr. Zoditch.

ZODITCH

And what else?

FEATHERS

Nothing else, sir.

ZODITCH

But she was anxious?

FEATHERS

I don't know, sir.

ZODITCH

She seemed excited, nervous?

FEATHERS

I couldn't say, sir.

ZODITCH

You are a stupid little girl. When I am master of this house I will not tolerate stupid servants, mark my words. I will not tolerate smiling. If you do not wish to live in the chimney do not trifle with me.

FEATHERS

Are you then to be master of this house, Mr. Zoditch?

[ 116 ]

ZODITCH

(*Thinking about something and not particularly listening*)
Eh?

FEATHERS

Are you to be the new master, sir?

ZODITCH

What have *you* heard?

FEATHERS

Nothing, sir.

ZODITCH

(*Grabbing the girl*)
You heard something. Out with it. Do not play games. She
mentioned my name to you?

FEATHERS

Oh yes, Mr. Zoditch. That she has.

ZODITCH

Ah. I knew it. In what connection?

FEATHERS

In connection with the weather, sir. She said this morning
that you left the house without your scarf.

ZODITCH

She noticed that, did she? (FEATHERS *nods head*) Well?
Well? What else did she say?

[ 117 ]

FEATHERS

(*Hesitantly*)

She said that only a fool walks in this weather without a scarf about his neck.


ZODITCH

A fool! You did not hear her correctly. Her manner? She did not perhaps rest her hand upon her cheek . . . (FEATHERS *shakes her head*) or tilt her head, thus . . . (FEATHERS *still shakes her head*) or utter any oohs or ahhhs?

(*Girl's face lights up and she nods her head*)


FEATHERS

Something of that, sir. An ooooh.


ZODITCH

Ah. Ah. (*Rubs his hands together and then anxiously shoos his hands at the girl*) Go. Go. Tell your mistress I shall be down shortly. (*The girl starts to go*) Wait. Just say I shall be down. Do not say shortly. (*She exits. To himself*) Shortly implies haste. Here there is no haste. A wormy apple is not to be thrown out, nor to be hastened to. (*Goes over to his closet and starts looking at his clothes. Picks a gray suit*) Gray. Neither too gaudy nor too funereal. Gray as a seagull.

(*He pulls it out and inspects it. He starts to brush it off. He is plainly thinking. From the darkened part of the room, in his imagination, a voice*)


KATERINA

Will you have a piece of fudge, Mitya? (ZODITCH *turns without surprise. He is going to act out his approach to the woman.*

[ 118 ]

*This is how he imagines it will be. As he turns, the couch area lights up and we see* KATERINA PROLOMNAYA. *She is an immense woman, a good four or five inches taller than* ZODITCH. *She is overstuffed, overripe, and yet sensual for it all. Her face is heavily painted, her hair is intricately in place with hairpins. He takes the proffered fudge and sits down on the couch. They both eat fudge while staring intently at each other*) Do you like the fudge, Mitya?

ZODITCH

It is only fudge, Katerina. I do not concern myself with fudge. A man concerns himself with taxes, estates, properties, and bank balances.

KATERINA
(*Sighing*)
I know. I know. But surely there must be time for . . . (*Hesitantly*) other things.

ZODITCH

Other things? I do not understand what you mean by other things. (*Points to match*) The match.

KATERINA

Yes, Mitya. (*She lights his cigar*) I enjoy a man smoking a cigar.

ZODITCH

Your late husband did not smoke?

KATERINA

No.

ZODITCH

That is unfortunate. A house without tobacco smoke is a house not lived in.

KATERINA

Yes, that is true. (*Then a bit too forward*) Oh, Mitya, these last few months have been lonely ones for me. Knowing that you were near and yet so distant.

ZODITCH
(*Raises his hand*)
You must learn to keep your lusts under control, Katerina. The ashtray, please. (*She hands him the ashtray*) A woman who cannot keep her lusts under control soon finds her lusts keep her under control. Lust is the devil's monastery on the road to hell.

KATERINA

The seas have been rough for me, Mitya. Women by their nature are but frail vessels. They only have their hearts to guide them.

ZODITCH

And so I have come to consider taking the helm.

KATERINA

Oh, Mitya.

ZODITCH

To *consider*, Katerina. *Consider*. To consider is not to undertake; it is merely to consider.

[ 120 ]

KATERINA

(*A bit subdued*)

Yes.


ZODITCH

Yet many things are finally arrived at which, at first, were but considered.


KATERINA

(*Her hopes picking up*)

Yes. Yes.


ZODITCH

As you know I am by nature and by inclination a bachelor. However, since the death of my dear mother who was constantly by my side these past thirty-five years, I have had the inclination to seek another who might be equally solicitous of my welfare. One who might be concerned to see, as it were, the proper socks laid out in the morning, the stove lit fifteen minutes before awakening, the washbasin filled with water neither too hot nor too cold and, as it were, et cetera, et cetera, et cetera. In brief, one who might so conform her life to mine that we become a single entity of one mind, of one direction. I, on the other hand, shall, as it were, seize the helm of our mutual fortunes and guide the ship all safely into harbor. A man can do no less than to captain his ship, a woman can do no more than obey. Nothing less is correct; nothing more permissible.


KATERINA

Is it then to be so nautical? What of love, Mitya?

[ 121 ]

ZODITCH

What of love! On the sea of marriage love is understood.

KATERINA

(*Taking his hand and stroking it*)
Our love, Mitya?

ZODITCH

Our love! Any love! There is no need to bring up superfluous topics. We must proceed logically. The disorganized mind is the handmaiden of cupidity. (*Pulls a sheet of paper out of his pocket. From this point on she slowly but surely begins making physical overtures*) Now. My bill of assets. What you may expect in terms of physical property. (*Places the paper before her. She leans close*) Three pairs of shoes. Two in excellent condition. One in used condition, though without holes. Seven pairs of black socks. The wash, therefore, must be done no later than the sixth day of every week. (*She puts her hand on his ankle*) There is no need to inspect the socks at this time. Everything is as I will state it. (*Proceeds with the inventory. She moves in on him by degrees as he recites his list of assets*) Three suits: one black, one brown, one gray. Eighteen pieces of undergarments. In undergarments I am particularly fortunate, having received twelve pieces in total settlement of my late cousin's estate. Five shirts, four cotton white, one Egyptian cotton striped. A wool overcoat, full cut with imitation pearl buttons. A malacca cane belonging to the estate of my late father, still in the process of settlement, but to which I have indisputable right; a Persian rug, nine by twelve, purchased for me by my departed mother in Constantinople; bedding supplies consisting of two sheets, two pillow cases, one pillow and a six-inch-thick Siberian goose-down comforter.

KATERINA

And your heart, Mitya?

ZODITCH

(*Pulling out a bank book*)

A bank statement, listing monetary assets in excess of one hundred seventeen rubles.

KATERINA

And your heart, Mitya? Your heart?

ZODITCH

What are you talking about? We are itemizing now!

KATERINA

(*Grown increasingly amorous*)

I must have love. Love. Love.

ZODITCH

There is no place for love in an itemizing of particulars. Where is your list of physical property?

KATERINA

(*Grabs his hand and places it on her heart*)

Here is my physical property. Feel it beating.

ZODITCH

Where is your bill of purchase for the house? Your list of bank holdings? Your movables? Your tangibles and intangibles?

KATERINA

My dogs, Mitya, what of my dogs?

[ 123 ]

ZODITCH

Superfluous. To be gotten rid of. I am not piloting a dog-house.

KATERINA

Be my pilot. Mine.
(*Shoves some fudge practically into his mouth*)

ZODITCH

Show me the bills of purchase. How many horses are in the stable. I don't want any fudge. (*She puts the fudge halfway into her mouth and begins to crawl all over him. She wants him to take the other half in his mouth. He retreats along the couch until there is no room to retreat. She literally begins physically overpowering him. She presses the fudge against his mouth until he starts biting it. His conversation until he devours the fudge runs something like*) What are you doing? Why are you touching me? You're pushing me. Listen. Don't. Wait. How much is your bank balance? What are you doing? Don't come any closer. You're hurting me. Let me up. Up. Up. Up.
(*When he does take the fudge from her mouth into his, he starts chewing it up furiously. Now she does the talking*)

KATERINA

We will have our honeymoon in the house. We will stay in the bedroom. There will be no need for you to work. No need to ever leave the house. We will raise the rents. (*She grabs his head and forces him to kiss her*) Don't kiss me so hard, Mitya, not yet, not yet. I want to make love to you. Yes. Oh make love to me always. Always. Never leave the house. Pa-

[ 124 ]

tience, Mitya, not yet. Wait until we are man and wife. Be sweet. Be gentle. Never leave the house.

ZODITCH

Let me go. For the love of God. You're crushing me. I can't breathe. You're crushing me.

KATERINA

Kiss me, Mitya. Put your arms around me. Crush me. Crush me.

ZODITCH

Get off. Off.

(*He suddenly frees himself from her embrace and flees to his desk. Lights out on the couch. He stands shakily by his desk trying to catch his breath. Suddenly, from down below there comes the voice of* KATERINA PROLOMNAYA *in the midst of the barking of dogs*)

KATERINA
(*Shouting*)

If you're coming down, Zoditch, come down! I haven't all night to spend waiting for you!
(*Followed by wild barking*)

ZODITCH
(*Wildly to himself, almost tearfully*)

Yes. Yes. Good-bye, Miss Grubov. Good-bye. (*Out loud*) Yes. Yes. I'm coming, Katerina Prolomnaya. I'm coming. (*Runs over to the closet and slips into the gray trousers*) Coming. Coming. (*Throws on the coat, grabs the diary and some official papers. He stamps them with a seal*) With a seal. Official.

[ 125 ]

(*Starts to read as he runs out*) I'm coming, Katerina Prolomnaya. Coming.

(*Light dims on* ZODITCH'S *room but does not go out. Lights up on* CHULKATURIN *standing in the entrance to the* OZHOGIN *living room.* KIRILLA *is warmly welcoming him. He rushes up and puts his arms around* CHULKATURIN)

#### KIRILLA

Ah, my friend, you have come. In spite of everything you have come. (*To* VOLOBRINA) Bring some tea for our guest. Quickly. (*Embraces* CHULKATURIN *again as* VOLOBRINA *heads for kitchen*) Come in. Come in. Let me take your coat. (*Helps* CHULKATURIN *off with his coat*) Here, by the fire. Soon winter will be down upon us. You are well?

#### CHULKATURIN

Yes.

#### KIRILLA

Good. Good.

#### CHULKATURIN

And you and Madam Ozhogin?

#### KIRILLA

(*Opens his hands as a form of silent reply meaning, "As well as might be expected"*)
Well.

#### CHULKATURIN

And Liza?

[ 126 ]

KIRILLA

Ah. How quickly the summer has gone. How quickly youth
vanishes. Smoke, that is all it is, dear Chulkaturin, smoke and
expectations. This is a different household you have come into.

CHULKATURIN

You mustn't blame yourself.

KIRILLA

But they blame me, all of them, Anna, the servants. You
see what ingratitude is? Could I tell what a snake he was
when he came into this house. Is it every snake that walks
around and says he is a snake? But he never fooled you, my
dear friend. You knew him from the start. I saw no more than
the show of things, but you saw into the heart. You saw the
snake in the man.

CHULKATURIN

Has he written to her? (KIRILLA *shakes his head*) That is to
be expected. It is just as well.

KIRILLA

(*Slowly nodding his head*)

Yes. Just as well. Oh, my friend, what can I say to you? You
fought, you risked your life to save my daughter from him and
only received contempt in return. What can be said to you?

CHULKATURIN

Your friendship now is all I desire.

KIRILLA

You have that, my friend, from the bottom of my heart.

[ 127 ]

CHULKATURIN

And to bring Liza happiness.


KIRILLA

Ah, if that were only possible. If I could believe that you could find forgiveness for her.


CHULKATURIN

It is possible. I do forgive.


KIRILLA

(*Sinking into his chair. He is almost in tears*)
What irony. Bitter bitter irony. The whole town condemns her and you who have every right . . .


CHULKATURIN

I do not care what fools condemn. (*Sinks to his knees by* KIRILLA's *side and touches his hand*) You understand? She is not of less value to me because of fools.


KIRILLA

She is a young girl. She made a mistake. The judgment of the young is not foolproof.


CHULKATURIN

Yes. As you say. If she will have me even now I will marry her. I will take her to Lambswater. She will be loved as no woman has ever been loved. She will be respected. I swear that to you.


KIRILLA

(*Speechless*)
Respect? Is it yet possible?

[ 128 ]

Believe what I say, my friend. If you believe nothing else of me, believe that. Let the past be done.

CHULKATURIN

Believe what I say, my friend. If you believe nothing else of me, believe that. Let the past be done.

KIRILLA

(*Practically bursts into tears as he hugs him*)

You have her. You have her. I don't know what to . . . You have her! Go to her. She is alone in the garden . . . Go, my son. Take her. (*He releases* CHULKATURIN) Your coat. Don't catch cold. (*Gives* CHULKATURIN *his coat.* CHULKATURIN *stands in the doorway leading to the garden.* KIRILLA *flees the living room*) Anna! Anna!

(*Lights out on* CHULKATURIN. *Lights up on* ZODITCH *in the apartment of* KATERINA PROLOMNAYA. *She stands before a meat grinder, grinding meat. In the background we hear the intermittent growling of her dogs*)

ZODITCH

Katerina Prolomnaya, what is loneliness? Did not the Roman poets tell us, "Lupus pilum mutat, non mentem," meaning we are all thrust alone on a dark sea. (*Pauses expecting a response. There is none. He goes on*) A dark sea! A sea without light. A sea of gigantic waves. In life, Katerina Prolomnaya, the wind blows. The wind blows! (*Pauses for a second to wipe his forehead with a handkerchief*) And what is the effect of this wind? It pushes us along. We do not know where we have sailed from. We do not know where we sail to. We sail! (*Again he pauses, but still she continues grinding*) No man can say, "No, I will not sail. No, I will remain where I am safe." This he cannot say because the wind blows. That is the substance of it all—the wind. And what is the effect of this wind when we

sail in the darkness, Katerina Prolomnaya? Who's to say how
many of us are blown over the edges of the world. Which is
to say without metaphor, how many of us come to bad fortune
because he . . . or she . . . sailed alone. To sail alone is to
vanish alone. And this is the answer to my question, Katerina
Prolomnaya.

KATERINA

You have received the extra coal and oil I sent.

ZODITCH

(*Nervous. Wiping his forehead again*)
Yes, yes, thank you. We see that what is loneliness is to be
alone and to vanish alone. (*Softly, as if trying to remember a
set speech*) To vanish alone. (*Then a bit too loudly*) Loneliness must end! How is loneliness to end? Loneliness ends when
a light is lit.

KATERINA

(*Suddenly shouting at the dogs*)
Shut up!

ZODITCH

(*In a moment of sudden fright* ZODITCH *knocks a small
piece of meat off the table. He instantly bends down to
pick it up*)
Excuse me. Excuse me. (*Puts the meat back on the table.
He continues, nervously*) And what power do we have to strike
such a light? Mutual feeling . . . mutual regard, but even
more than this, love. Love is a light. When two boats come
together they make a light. This is the holy light of marriage.
Now we must ask, **what** is marriage? Marriage is a sacrament,

and by a sacrament the church means a sanctity and a union of spirits; therefore, marriage is not based on material possession. Oh, no, Katerina Prolomnaya, it is not a contract of assets and liabilities. The church does not intend us to inquire into the number of houses owned, the number of horses in the stable. Love is above these things. It makes a harmony from separateness. It makes joy. It is above rings and rubles. (*KATERINA has stopped grinding the meat and now stares directly at him. He has grown very nervous*) It is the light that moves above the darkness of the sea. It is the star and moon. It is the refuge, the shelter, the roof against the wind. (*Suddenly taking her hand. She continues trying to grind the meat. He continues trying to get her to stop. A silent grinding.* ZODITCH *is dismayed. Nevertheless he continues*) Know, dear Katrina Prolomnaya, that it was not for nothing that your extra coal to me was given. Know that such seeds of generosity, of goodness, did not fall on barren ground, but that they found their way to this heart that even now illuminates with respectful fondness.

KATERINA

Now that you have been advanced in your position you will pay me two extra rubles a month for coal and oil.

ZODITCH

To you, Katerina, I offer this hand of marriage, this hand of spiritual bondage, this hand . . .

KATERINA

I cannot marry you. You are too old, too . . . (*Looking at him up and down*) short.

(*Light slowly fades out on* KATERINA PROLOMNAYA)

[ 131 ]

ZODITCH

(*Turns and faces the audience*)

Too old? *I* am too old. It is *I* who am laughing, Katerina Prolomnaya. (*Laughs a dry hollow laugh*) I laugh to think you can laugh at me. It is you who are the wrinkled fish here. (*Cups his hand to his ear*) Is that so? Is that so, madam? Well, it is I who stoop to consider marriage to you. I laugh in your face. I withdraw my offer . . . When I marry Miss Grubov your tongue will hang out to come to the wedding. (*From somewhere in his mind comes the sound of* KATERINA *laughing*) You keep your dogs away from me, Katerina Prolomnaya. Your tongue will hang out to be invited. Get away you filthy beasts. Get away. (*He begins kicking at invisible dogs*) To a man of my position your assets are nothing. I am not interested in your buildings and your rents. I am a man of sensibilities. A man interested in love and feelings. Get away from my legs, you bitches. I'll kick your heads in. You think I didn't know the coal was given just to raise my rent? Keep your coal and kerosene. (*Laughter breaks out again*) What did you expect for a husband? A giant? Jack and the beanstalk? A ten-foot monster? There is no golden goose for you. You are no princess of the pea. Get away. Leave me alone. I'll kill you, you bitches. I'll kill you. Gregory! Gregory! Madhouse. Madhouse. Madhouse!

(*Lights dim on* ZODITCH *frozen in a scream.*

*Lights up on* LIZA *and* BIZMIONKOV *in the garden.*

CHULKATURIN *stands half unseen in the archway*)

LIZA

How brown the garden has become. How dry.

BIZMIONKOV

Perhaps the captain will yet write.

LIZA

You think so? (*Catching herself*) No. It is done. He will not write. Ivan Petrovich has gone to Petersburg and he will not write. Shall I dig up these flowers do you think, and bring them inside? They will die in the first snow.

BIZMIONKOV

Let them die, Liza.

LIZA

Papa must have taken the spade inside. I cannot seem to find it.

BIZMIONKOV

What of Chulkaturin?

LIZA

(*Suddenly stops looking for the spade. She speaks with scorn*)

That one? How hateful that name sounds to me. (*Touching some flowers*) These petals are still soft. I can save these flowers.

BIZMIONKOV

He has not left yet.

LIZA

Ah. Still he waits. For what does he wait? To forgive me? I do not need his forgiveness. Better that he had never known my brother. Better that the door to this house had remained forever shut against him.

BIZMIONKOV

He is in love with you.

LIZA

His love is nothing to me now! I cannot forgive him. What did he want here? Did he come all this way to stand alone at dances? To throw flowers to no one? To shoot Ivan? For what did he come?

BIZMIONKOV
(*Slowly*)

I think Nikolai Alexeevich Chulkaturin came all this way to love you.

LIZA
(*There is a pause in which she looks at* BIZMIONKOV *for a long time, as if seeing him for the first time*)

How good you are. You are an angel. What should I have ever done without you?

BIZMIONKOV

Is there nothing then for Chulkaturin?

LIZA

I have forgotten him. (*Raising her hands to his face*) My friend, if you love me, knowing all, I will do as you ask. I will become your wife.

(BIZMIONKOV *embraces her, slowly, tightly.* CHULKA-TURIN *lets out a short cry*)

[ 134 ]

CHULKATURIN

You, Bizmionkov? You?

ZODITCH

No, Miss Grubov! Not Pandalevski! (*Lights go out on* BIZ-MIONKOV *and* LIZA. ZODITCH *and* CHULKATURIN *are left facing each other across the stage.* ZODITCH *grabs the manuscript in his hand*) This is a story of lies! You are a liar! You distort. Do you see what I am doing? I reject this manuscript. I reject you.
(*Writing across the face of the manuscript*)

CHULKATURIN

And I stood in the garden dumb and dark with hedges, stood as if winds of a thousand centuries might wash upon me and find me standing yet. And for all of it, the roses shut in books, the crowns of May, the duels, the summer dances, what for all of it, if, at the last, to say, "Bizmionkov, is it you?"
(*Extends his arm to* ZODITCH)

ZODITCH

Liar! I am the one that is loved! That is the ending. I am loved! (*There is a pause in which* ZODITCH *and* CHULKATURIN *stare at each other. When* ZODITCH *speaks the anger has been replaced by anguish*) What do you want of me? (CHULKA-TURIN's *arm falls. Lights out on* CHULKATURIN. ZODITCH, *with rage, throws the diary violently away*) I am the one that is loved. There is no other ending.
(*He begins curling himself up into a hard ball as if suddenly very cold.*
*Lights out*)

**VOICE**

And when I had passed through the antique marketplace of Samarkand, through the cries and fevers of the merchants, the monkey's hand fell within his cage, and there was nothing further to the matter.

**CURTAIN**

# Harry, Noon and Night

## A Play in Three Scenes

They said, "You have a blue guitar,
You do not play things as they are."
The man replied, "Things as they are
Are changed upon the blue guitar."

WALLACE STEVENS

# The Original Cast

(*in order of appearance*)

| | |
|---|---|
| HARRY | Joel Grey |
| SOLDIER | Richard Schaal |
| PROSTITUTE | Lynn Bernay |
| ARCHER | Gerald S. O'Loughlin |
| IMMANUEL | Dustin Hoffman |
| HERMAN (*offstage voice*) | |
| HERMAN'S WIFE | Lotte Stavisky |
| POLICEMAN | Bruce Glover |

The first performance of *Harry, Noon and Night* was given on March 17, 1965, at the American Place Theatre in New York City. It was directed by George Morrison. Scenery, lighting, and costumes were by Robert Mitchell.

SCENE ONE

**Harry** entertains a soldier from Nashville

The Dolly Bar: late afternoon


SCENE TWO

Immanuel entertains a visitor from Ohio

**Harry and Immanuel's room:** the same afternoon


SCENE THREE

**To divide** what is thine from what is mine

**Harry** and Immanuel's room: 10:30 that night


TIME:   December 1955

PLACE:   Munich, Germany

# Scene One

*Harry entertains a soldier from Nashville*

PLACE: *The Dolly bar in Munich, Germany.*

TIME: *December 1955, late one afternoon.*

SCENE: *A small round table and three chairs. **On the table** are several beer bottles, glasses, and ashtrays littered with cigarette butts. Upstage, left, is a very scraggly Christmas tree, interlaced with small electric-light bulbs and beaten-up ornaments. Offstage, a jukebox is playing "Hark, the Herald Angels Sing."*

ON RISE: HARRY *and a* SOLDIER *are sitting on opposite sides of the table. Between them and facing the audience is a young, attractive German* PROSTITUTE.

HARRY, *about twenty-five, is industriously writing in a child's notebook. The* SOLDIER, *several years younger, is kissing the* GIRL's *neck.*

*Throughout the scene, the* PROSTITUTE *is mechanical in her movements, as if nothing that goes on has anything to do with her. She smokes, drinks, looks about for future customers, advertises her body, keeps time to melodies heard and unheard. She moves to her own rhythm.* HARRY *and the* SOLDIER *regard her more as an object than as a human being. Whenever it pleases them they fondle her.*

[ 143 ]

*They run their hands over her legs, her breasts, and they never miss a beat in their conversation.*

*As* HARRY *continues writing, the* GIRL *puts her arms around the* SOLDIER *and begins warming him up, literally crawling all over him.*

*While the music plays, the* SOLDIER *and the* PROSTITUTE *continue this lovemaking. When the music stops,* HARRY *speaks. He does so without looking up as he continues writing.*

HARRY

Do you have to do that? (*Neither the* SOLDIER *nor the* GIRL *seems to have heard.* HARRY *writes a bit more. This time when he speaks it is startlingly loud*) Do you?

SOLDIER
(*As if coming out of a trance*)
Huh? What's the matter?

HARRY
(*Imitating his words and facial expression*)
Huh? What? Huh?

SOLDIER
What's the matter, man?

HARRY
(*Sharply*)
This is what's the matter, man. (*He slowly pulls the* GIRL *over to him and begins kissing the* GIRL's *throat and running his hands over her body. She begins to respond to him just as she had to the* SOLDIER. *The* SOLDIER *is plainly embarrassed*)
Do you have to do that?

[ 144 ]

SOLDIER

I thought you wanted to write awhile.

HARRY

How am I supposed to write? Here . . . (*Shoves book and pencil at him*) You write. (HARRY *goes into a noisy parody of the* SOLDIER's *lovemaking technique. The* SOLDIER, *dumfounded, stares at the book and pencil*) Go on, write!

SOLDIER

What?

HARRY

Anything. The pledge to the flag. Dixieland. (SOLDIER *just sits there while* HARRY *continues to mock his lovemaking technique. The noises grow more and more passionate and animalistic*) Can't be done, can it? (SOLDIER *mumbles something.* HARRY *cups his hand to his ear*) Eh? Eh? What's that?

SOLDIER

No.

HARRY

(*Stops his necking parody*)

You bet your ass it can't be done. (SOLDIER *is nervously trying to light a cigarette*) You think I'm blind? I mean you sit there running your tongue along her neck, blowing into her ear, and she's wiggling her breasts all around and snaking up against you and all them goddam sucking sounds and hot breathing. What am I supposed to do? Ignore it? (*The* SOLDIER *is thoroughly chastened.* HARRY *stares at him and then looks back at his notes*) Where was I?

[ 145 ]

SOLDIER

The blue braid in my hat.

HARRY

(*Puts the notebook and pencil down in disgust*)
I don't know. I lost my whole train of thought.

SOLDIER

I think you wanted me to tell you about the braid.

HARRY

That's not the point. I lose track of one thing I forget about
everything. That's the kind of mind I got. One interruption and
I can't remember beans. I'm the only one in my family like
that.

SOLDIER

(*He has grown even more uncomfortable*)
I'm pretty sure we were up to the braid.

HARRY

(*Stares off into the blue and then suddenly shouts*)
Let's go with the jukebox. Play something with Christ in it.
Let's put Christ back in Germany. What do you think we're
here for? (*He pulls the* SOLDIER *toward him and loudly whis-
pers*) This is confidential. (*Winks*) Entre nous, you know what
I mean? Why, with a palaceful of queens, do you wanna have
at it with just this princess? (SOLDIER *shrugs, extending his
palms up.* HARRY *tries again as if eliciting a great secret*) Come
on. What's the story? (SOLDIER *shrugs in the same fashion.*
HARRY *becomes annoyed and imitates* SOLDIER's *motions*) What's
that mean? What's it, a code or something?

SOLDIER

No, man.

(HARRY *nudges him in a secretive way*)

HARRY

What's the story?

SOLDIER

You're not going to put this in the article, are you? If my
mother read . . .

HARRY

(*Loudly*)

Whoa! Whoa! (*Then confidentially*) This is for me, off the
record. What we writers call entre nous. It goes in my files and
they can't be subpoenaed. (SOLDIER *nods head*) You see, *American Farm and Garden* is for mothers. In a hundred years there
hasn't been one article in *American Farm and Garden* about
soldiers getting laid. The American mother doesn't want to
read about it. We wanna keep America clean. You're for that,
aren't you?

SOLDIER

Yeah.

HARRY

(*Rests back content. There is a moment of silence*)
Well?

SOLDIER

Huh?

[ 147 ]

HARRY

Why do you want to have at it with this one in particular?


SOLDIER

I don't know.


HARRY

Of course you know. What's the story? (SOLDIER *sits there nervously fidgeting*) You find her witty, clever?


SOLDIER

She doesn't speak English.


HARRY

Her personality. You like her personality? (SOLDIER *shrugs noncommittally.* HARRY *slices through the pretense. Grabs the* GIRL's *breasts*) The va-va-vooms. Is it the va-va-vooms?


SOLDIER
(*Shyly*)

I don't know.


HARRY

You know! You know!


SOLDIER

It's kind of funny to explain. (*He hopes* HARRY *will let it go at this.* HARRY *just keeps staring at him*) It changes from week to week. (HARRY *continues to stare*) It changes. Sometimes I like a girl . . .

   (SOLDIER *indicates with his hands that sometimes he likes a girl with big breasts. He is too embarrassed to put it bluntly, but* HARRY *won't let him get away with it. He mimics the* SOLDIER'S *gesture*)

HARRY

What's this? (SOLDIER *is quiet*) Big va-va-vooms?
(SOLDIER *nods*)

SOLDIER

Sometimes it's other parts.

HARRY

What other parts?

SOLDIER

Other parts.

HARRY

The legs? (SOLDIER *still shakes head*) Well, what the hell you on this week? Hair? Arms? Toes? Crotch? (HARRY *suddenly stands the* GIRL *up, whirls her around. Finally her back faces the audience.* GIRL *smooths out dress along her buttocks. They stare silently for a moment while the* GIRL *emphasizes that asset*) That's what you're on this week. Right? Right? (SOLDIER *doesn't say anything, but you can see* HARRY *is right.* HARRY *turns to* GIRL) Here, put it in the jukebox. I wanna hear something with Jesus in it.

(*Gives her money. She walks offstage wiggling all the way. Before she leaves, the* SOLDIER *nervously calls after*)

SOLDIER

You come back right after. You understand? Versteh? Here!
(*She goes offstage*)

[ 149 ]

HARRY

Okay, let's get back to work. You were on the blue cord. (SOLDIER *is still looking after the* GIRL) Look, I only got so much time. If you don't want the money for paradise, just let me know and I'll get somebody else to interview.

SOLDIER

No, man, I need that money bad. I've been waiting for her since Thanksgiving.

HARRY

Okay, then. Let's go with the blue string.

SOLDIER

You shouldn't have sent her to the jukebox. They ain't reliable like the girls back home. Somebody's gonna pick her up. (*Looks after the* GIRL. *Turns to* HARRY) Maybe I oughta . . . (*Indicates he wants to go after.* HARRY *gives him a nasty look and the* SOLDIER *realizes he'd better continue*) The blue cord in the hat is for the infantry. And the blue braid here . . . (*Points to a cord running through the epaulet of the shoulder*) . . . also means infantry. This crest . . . (SOLDIER *leans across the table so* HARRY *can get a closer look at the crest on the epaulet*) . . . is the battalion crest, "Courage Conquers." Can you see that?

HARRY

(*Squints at it, keeps revolving it around presumably to catch the light, pulls at the epaulet*)
What the hell's that supposed to mean? Conquers what?

SOLDIER

It's the battalion crest.

[ 150 ]

HARRY

But what the hell does it mean?

SOLDIER

It doesn't mean anything. It's just the battalion crest. Every battalion has its own motto, see?
(*Looks around for the* GIRL)

HARRY

Every battalion got a different motto?

SOLDIER

Yeah. (*Still looking. Then, practically in anguish*) I don't hear the jukebox.

HARRY

Like what?

SOLDIER

Huh?

HARRY

Like what? Like what? What other mottoes?

SOLDIER

Man, I don't know. You don't go around memorizing those things.

HARRY

Listen, you said you were gonna be honest and open with me. That's the American way. Don't be a clown.

[ 151 ]

SOLDIER

I am being honest and open. You don't go around memorizing . . .

HARRY

Wait a minute. (*Starts digging around in his pockets. He mumbles*) Honest and open, huh.

SOLDIER

Man, I *know* what I signed.

HARRY

Just a minute.

(*Keeps searching*)

SOLDIER

But I remember what I . . .

HARRY

Can you wait just that minute? Just that minute? (*Pulling it out*) Here, read it. (SOLDIER *wearily takes it and stares at it*) Out loud.

SOLDIER

(*Reading as fast as possible*)

"I do solemnly swear to Harry to tell the truth, the whole truth and nothing but the truth to Harry so help me God." I am telling the truth, Harry. Lemme think.

(*Raises his hand to get a second's peace.* HARRY *doesn't give it to him*)

HARRY

That's the American way. Every magazine writer in America has to get his information sources to sign that pledge of truth.

It's the only way we have of knowing that what we're told is the truth, the whole truth, and nothing but the truth. Nothing can be printed unless that pledge is signed. If I were interviewing the President of the United States he'd have to sign that pledge. You know that? Even the President!

SOLDIER
(*Thinks for a moment*)
"Men of Blood," that's one motto for the 356th Airborne. "To the Death" is another. That's all I can remember.

HARRY
There was a soldier in here last week whose battalion crest said "Sur le pont d'Avignon." What outfit's that?

SOLDIER
Said what?

HARRY
"Sur le Pont d'Avignon."

SOLDIER
I never heard of that outfit. (HARRY *stares at him in disbelief*) I never heard of that outfit!

HARRY
Okay. Just don't clown around with me. What's that check mark on your sleeve?

SOLDIER
(*In surprise, pointing to his PFC chevron*)
This? (HARRY *nods*) Man, how can you be writing an article about Army life and know so little?

[ 153 ]

HARRY

That's why I'm talking to you. What do you think I'm paying you money for? You want the money or don't you want the money? (*Pause that is almost a contest of wills.* SOLDIER *gives in by nodding his head*) All right. What's the story with those check marks?

SOLDIER

They're chevrons. They tell rank. I'm a PFC, that's a private first class. (SOLDIER *is looking around, then suddenly*) Oh, man, you know what she's doing? She went out for a quickie.

HARRY

The ones with two check marks are privates second class?

SOLDIER

They're corporals. You don't know the kind of women they got around here. Shut your eyes for a second and they're on their back with three other guys, humping away like there was no tomorrow.

HARRY

The ones without stripes are privates second class?

SOLDIER

They're just privates.

HARRY

(*Exasperated*)

Then who's a private second class?

SOLDIER

(*More exasperated*)

There ain't no private second class.

HARRY

(*Most exasperated*)

Then what the hell do they have to have private first classes
for?

SOLDIER

Man, you got this thing all confused. I don't know where to
begin. (*Switches topic. Starts mumbling about the* GIRL) They
don't give a damn about who they sleep with. If a gorilla bust
outta the zoo they'd sleep with him. You know that? Just as
long as he had the money. That's all.

HARRY

What's that horse manure on your chest?

SOLDIER

Aw, don't call it that, man. It's ribbons and decorations . . .
Christ! Right out for a quickie.

(*Slaps hands together and slides them off each other,
and then starts nodding his head up and down*)

HARRY

What's that one?

SOLDIER

The National Defense Ribbon. You get that when you're in
the service four months.

HARRY

You mean they give you a ribbon just because you've been sucking around for four months?

SOLDIER

It's for active duty. It's nothing to do with sucking around.

HARRY

Listen, I'm taking this down. If you're feeding me a load of horsefeathers . . .
(*He starts searching for the oath.* SOLDIER *grabs his hand*)

SOLDIER

Oh, man, not the oath thing again. I'm giving it to you straight arrow.

HARRY

Okay. I'm relying on you. I can't write an article that's full of cow-crap. You feed me cow-crap and they'll fire me. I got a kid that's stone blind depending on me. He sits in a roachy apartment all day depending on me.

SOLDIER

Oh, sweet Jesus.

HARRY

Not too many people know about it.

SOLDIER

What's the name of that magazine?

HARRY

*American Farm and Garden.*

SOLDIER

(*Nods head*)

Well, I'm giving you the truth.

HARRY

What's that one for?

SOLDIER

The European Occupation Medal. You get that for being
here during the time of occupation.

HARRY

Occupying what?

SOLDIER

Germany.

HARRY

Are you sure about that? My brother Archer was here when
they were fighting hand to hand in the streets and I don't recall him getting any occupying medals.

SOLDIER

When was that?

HARRY

Nineteen forty-four.

[ 157 ]

SOLDIER

Well they weren't occupying then. They were still fighting, see?

HARRY

Archer was in the Air Force. Got a Congressional Medal for strafing. He kept strafing and strafing. That was his specialty. He could keep strafing and strafing at things until they crumbled.

(*Lapses into self-thought*)

SOLDIER

Well, that would explain it. You gotta be in the Army to get an occupation medal. The Air Force flies over. You gotta be on the ground.

HARRY

(*Snaps out of it*)

Are you sure about this being the Army of Occupation?

SOLDIER

Sure, I'm sure about it. What do you think they got all these soldiers here for? This is the Army of Occupation.

HARRY

I'm writing that down, so if you're feeding me a wagonload of mule shit . . .

SOLDIER

Go on, put my name down. It's the truth. My name's Humphrey Hill.

HARRY

Okay, I'm gonna do that. I'm quoting you.

SOLDIER

Go ahead. (HARRY *starts writing. The* GIRL *returns and sits down. The* SOLDIER *stares at her, trying to make up his mind if she went out with another* SOLDIER. *She begins adjusting herself: her dress, her hair, her makeup*) She's all mussed up!

HARRY

You spell Hill with an I or an E?

SOLDIER

(*Impatiently spells it out*)

H-I-L-L. Look how mussed up she is. (HARRY *goes back to his writing.* SOLDIER *begins a detailed inspection of the* GIRL) The lipstick's smeared. The mascara's running. The zipper is open halfway down her back. (*Sticks his head under the table*) One of the garters is unhooked! Man, I tell you, you send them off to jukeboxes and they're down on their backs, arms and legs flailing all over. They have no morals. One second and rummmmmm. (*Makes sound of a racing car zooming by. To* GIRL) You sleep with people one at a time, not in groups. (*Sticks his hand inside front of blouse*) Oh, man, they tore the strap. Oh, man. (*He is real sorrowful, as if his own private property has been damaged. He keeps trying to fix the strap, while he moans*) Oh, man, let's meet tomorrow and finish this. Give me the forty Marks now and I'll meet you tomorrow, anywhere you say. Be a buddy, it's Christmas.

HARRY

Can't. Not enough time.

[ 159 ]

SOLDIER

Please, man.

HARRY

I gotta finish the article today. I'm booked on the track-four
night express to the Dachau circus. Fourteen dancing bears,
seven singing kangaroos, and Moko . . . Moko, the crying
clown. (*The* SOLDIER *just stares at him. Then the* SOLDIER *continues to fix the strap.* HARRY *looks up*) What's that ribbon for?

SOLDIER

Huh?

HARRY

Will you leave her boombos alone for a second?

SOLDIER

I'm listening.

HARRY

You're running your hands up and down her boombos. You're
playing footsie. You had your hand on her belly a minute ago.
You're doing everything but listening. (SOLDIER *is chastened*)
Now what is that purple and white piece of rag?

SOLDIER

This? It's blue.

(HARRY *grabs the row of decorations on the* SOLDIER'S
*chest and pulls them toward himself. He stares at them
from all angles, as if he can't make up his mind what color
it is*)

[ 160 ]

HARRY

You're right. Is that the Navy Cross?

SOLDIER

It's the Italian Campaign Medal! I'm in the Army! The battalion I'm in, the 370th Armored Infantry, fought in Italy during the Second World War and they gave this medal to the battalion to commemorate that action.

HARRY

You were fighting in the Second World War?

SOLDIER

Not me, personally. I was a kid then.

HARRY

Then what the hell you doing sucking up medals for battles you never fought in.

SOLDIER

I don't have to have fought in the Italian campaign. They gave the medal to the entire battalion and now everybody in the battalion wears it.

HARRY

Everybody? (SOLDIER *nods his head*) You mean the whole sucking battalion is going around with World War Two medals for battles they never been in? What kind of sheep dip you feeding me? You expect me to believe that? You really expect me to believe . . . This is going into a mothers' magazine. It has to be accurate. Let me tell you something. Do you know who the editors of *American Farm and Garden* are? Three women.

Two sisters and a mother. Each one is a worse son of a bitch than the other. They have chin whiskers, all three of them, and they catch me in one mistake, that's it, out . . . oh, you, tee, out. My kid is stone blind!

SOLDIER

I'm telling the truth. Man, I don't know what to do with you. I swear I'm telling you the truth.

HARRY

You're sure?

SOLDIER

Yeah.

HARRY

You swear?

(*He starts digging around for the pledge. The* SOLDIER *reaches out and holds his arm*)

SOLDIER

Please, man, I already swore.

HARRY

Because I'm quoting you. I got your name down here. (*Shows him the book*) Angler.

SOLDIER

My name is Hill! Lemme see that. (HARRY *holds onto book but lets him see it. Studies quote*) You got that quote wrong. I didn't say that.

(HARRY *snatches book back and looks at it*)

HARRY

Are you Hill or Angler?

SOLDIER

Hill. I told you before. Don't you remember? You asked if it was spelled with an I or an E.

HARRY

You didn't say the military around here was just sucking up the taxpayer's money?

SOLDIER

No, man, no! I never said that. You got the quotes mixed up between me and this Angler guy.

HARRY

You deny you said that?

SOLDIER

Yeah. I deny it.

HARRY

Okay, I'll take your word. I'm relying on you. I'm crossing it out. I'm giving you another chance.
(*Starts crossing out*)

SOLDIER
(*Shaking head*)

Man, they should've given you another assignment. Something else.

HARRY

Why do you say that? Don't you think I'm competent?

[ 163 ]

SOLDIER

It's not that.


HARRY

I've written lots of articles on the military. You ever hear of
*The Brothers Karamazov?* (SOLDIER *shakes head*) I wrote that.
*Wuthering Heights?* (SOLDIER *shakes head*) I wrote that, too.


SOLDIER

You ever been in the Army?


HARRY

What makes you ask that? Do I look like a draft dodger to
you?


SOLDIER

I was just asking.


HARRY

I wanted to go. They wouldn't take me. I got syphilis. I stood
in the goddam rain in front of the draft board for two hours
and they wouldn't take me. Whole town came down to see me
off. Even my brother who won the Congressional Medal for
strafing came around. He and his old buddies borrowed a
brace of P–51's and strafed over the draft board while I was
waiting in the rain. Whole town turned out. The doctor from
the draft board read the medical report out on the street. My
mother passed out from embarrassment.


SOLDIER

You gotta watch who you sleep around with.

HARRY

I did. I did. I watched all the time.


SOLDIER

Didn't you know she had syphilis?


HARRY

Huh? What are you talking about?


SOLDIER

The girl you slept with.


HARRY

What's girls got to do with this?


SOLDIER

Man, some girl gave it to you.


HARRY

The syphilis?

SOLDIER

That's where you got it from.


HARRY

What are you talking about? I got it from a caterpillar. It was on a toilet seat and bit me. (SOLDIER *shaking his head violently*) Whatta ya shaking your head?


SOLDIER

Listen, man, I don't know where you've been getting your medical information from, but they been feeding you a pack of lies. I bet you ain't got syphilis at all.

HARRY

Whatta ya talking about? The goddam fang marks. You wanna see them?

SOLDIER

It ain't possible to get syphilis from a caterpillar.

HARRY

The thing was right on a toilet seat. (SOLDIER *just sits there shaking his head*) Will you stop that? Will you?

SOLDIER

It ain't possible. Listen, man, they're too small to have sexual relations with. (HARRY *stares at him.* SOLDIER *changes topic. Points to ribbon*) You wanna know what this one's for?

HARRY

I wanted to serve. You better believe it. I woulda done anything to get behind Old Glory. I wanted to be a fighter pilot.

SOLDIER

This is the Good Conduct Ribbon.

HARRY

You ever had syphilis?

SOLDIER

I told you I was a Baptist.
(HARRY *begins writing furiously. The jukebox blares out* "The Stars and Stripes Forever." *The* GIRL *begins shaking all over and running her hands over the* SOLDIER. *She pulls*

[ 166 ]

*the* SOLDIER *to his feet and they dance sexually, provoca-
tively. The* GIRL *is blatantly advertising her wares to the*
SOLDIER. *After a few moments of writing,* HARRY *looks up*)

HARRY

What the hell's happening here? (*He gets up, grabs the* SOL-
DIER *and starts pulling him away. The* GIRL *keeps gyrating ob-
scenely. It gets to be a kind of tug of war between* HARRY, *who
tugs, and the* GIRL, *who makes open invitation*) Who gave the
signal for this? What's wrong with her body?

SOLDIER
(*Almost stunned*)
Oh, man, it's the music. I'm with it. I'm with it.

HARRY

That's "The Stars and Stripes" you're profaning. "The Stars
and Stripes"!

SOLDIER
Man, let me have the money. I'm movin'. I'm movin'.

HARRY
Don't dance that way in your country's uniform.

SOLDIER
Oh, man, oh, man.

HARRY
You're sullying your country. What about America? Is this
what the pilgrims died for? Is it? Why doesn't someone think

[ 167 ]

about America once in a while? Think about that. (*Pulls* SOL-
DIER *away from* GIRL) Leave go. This is a public place. Don't
look at her. Come on. Don't look at her. What about your
mother back in Nashville? Think about that. Don't look at her.

SOLDIER

Oh, man. I wanna get outta here.
   (HARRY *manages to separate them. He pulls the* SOLDIER
*back to the chair. The* GIRL *continues with her dance. The*
SOLDIER *tries to look.* HARRY *tries to stop him*)

HARRY

Remember your motto — "Courage Conquers"! Don't sully
that too. What's that bottle cap crud on your collar?

SOLDIER

Insignia. I wanna get out of here.

HARRY

What does U.S. stand for? Uncle Sam?

SOLDIER

U.S.! U.S.! Man, gimme the money, will ya? It's hours before
the night express goes. Lemme rip off a quick piece and then
I'll give you the rest of the article. That's all I want, a quick
piece.

HARRY

Not enough time.

SOLDIER

Ten minutes. Throw her right down on the bed. Ten minutes.
(*Music ends with a kind of boompt.* GIRL *stops in middle of*

*her movement.* SOLDIER *stares wildly about him. She returns to the table. Becomes impassive. Lights cigarette and blows smoke*) Look at that. They're all pairing off and leaving. Two and two, two and two. Eight minutes. I won't even throw the covers back.

HARRY

What's the blue disk?

SOLDIER

That's infantry blue. I told you before. The color of the in-fantry is blue! Two by two. It's biblical. It's Noah.

HARRY
(*Looks at his watch*)

What time is it?

SOLDIER
(*Looking at his own watch*)

Four o'clock.

HARRY

I'm going to adjust my watch to yours. Is that the exact time? (SOLDIER *nods his head*) My watch says seven o'clock. You sure it's not seven? I've got a train to catch.

SOLDIER

I set it by the radio.

HARRY

Well, that's the right time then. The radio clocks are never wrong. They set them by electromagnetic waves. Why's the color of the infantry blue?

SOLDIER

Oh, man. What do you mean, why? That's just the way things are. You gotta take things the way they are. Infantry is blue, artillery is red, armor is yellow. That's why I'm wearing a blue scarf. Everything is blue in the infantry. You see that guy over there?

HARRY

The one picking his nose?

SOLDIER

Nobody's picking his nose. The one over there.

HARRY

Way over there?

SOLDIER

Yeah. You see the scarf he's wearing?

HARRY

The orange one?

SOLDIER

It's yellow, man. Well, that's armor. And that guy over there . . .

HARRY

Where?

SOLDIER

Over there.

[ 170 ]

HARRY

Doing the dirty boogy?

SOLDIER

There ain't nobody doing the dirty boogy. Man, you see everything all wrong.

HARRY

What about him?

SOLDIER

He's in artillery. He's got a red scarf. Every branch got its individual color.

HARRY

How about branch socks?

SOLDIER

Jesus! Jesus H. Christ! You said you only wanted a few answers, but there's no end. You gonna go on and on and on.

HARRY

All the questions are written down here. (*Pointing to his papers*) Everything's organized. Every question is figured out in advance by electronic computers. Nothing's just made up. I got it down in columns.

SOLDIER

There's no branch socks. All the socks are brown.

HARRY

Everything's in columns. Why don't you have branch socks?

SOLDIER

Because they don't do things that way.

HARRY

Why not? You got blue scarfs and blue braids and blue john paper. Why not blue socks?

SOLDIER

They just don't do things that way. What are you talking about . . . blue toilet paper?

HARRY

How about blue underwear? You forgot about that.

SOLDIER

There's no blue underwear. They got regular white underwear.

HARRY

Well, how do they divide up what's supposed to be blue and what's not?

SOLDIER

(*Throws his arms up in the air*)

They must figure that out at higher headquarters. I don't know.

HARRY

(*Getting excited*)

Now we're really getting somewhere. This is going to be a real scoop, maybe even a lead article. (*Makes a point of writing this down*) "They figure that out at higher headquarters." Who's "they?"

[ 172 ]

SOLDIER

Huh?

HARRY

Who's the "they" that figure it out? (SOLDIER *raises his hands over his head again*) What is that supposed to be, Morse code?

(HARRY *imitates him by raising his hands over his head and shaking them.*)

SOLDIER

I don't know who "they" are, man. The leaders.

HARRY

I can't just put down "the leaders." I gotta have names. (*Suddenly*) The Secretary of Health, Education and Welfare is one, isn't he? (SOLDIER *shrugs*) Okay, we'll get back to that later. I'm gonna put that in Column A. This may be a scoop.

SOLDIER

Oh, man. Maybe we can do it after you come back from the Dachau circus. How about that?

HARRY

(*Said very seriously*)

I won't be coming back. Once I go I'm gone. (*Pause. Then* HARRY *jumps back into character*) What time is it now?

SOLDIER

Five after four.

HARRY

(*Stares mutely at his watch*)

I got five to four. My watch is going backwards. It's no good.

I never have the time. I told you about those bitches at the magazine. They keep me moving. I stay in one place a second too long and I get a cablegram. Last Thursday I thought I saw one of them looking for me. The worst bitch of all, the managing editor. I wasn't in the town a day. Listen, let me tell you. I haven't stopped moving for years. Three days in Thule, fourteen hours in Cairo, seventeen minutes between ships in Aden, and all the time I know they're keeping track of me. They have this big plotting board in the main office of *American Farm and Garden*. You know where that is? (SOLDIER *shakes his head*) Well, the general public doesn't know about it. It's in Westerville, Ohio. All the outside men like me are dots on that board. They know where we are every second. If we're a second too long in any place, the dot on the plotting board lights up and the field man is dispatched. If I don't get on that train tonight, my dot's gonna light up.

SOLDIER

So what? The hell with them.

(*He absentmindedly begins fondling the girl, but his eyes are on* HARRY. *He's absorbed in the story*)

HARRY

"So what," eh? Three lit-up dots in any one year and it's a black mark in the record files, and that's that. You can't erase it, and you can't wash it out, they never forget and they never forgive. Bitches all of them. They play us off, one against the other. That's the worst part of it. Every year for Christmas, you know what they do? (SOLDIER *shakes head. He almost casually, while listening, fondles* GIRL's *breast*) They cut one of us from the staff. Any one. We never know. They get us all together in

[ 174 ]

the main room on Christmas Eve and then they cut one of us from the staff. I got this stone-blind kid, but it won't make any difference to them. Bitches. So I gotta get everything straight. I can't put down any old horse manure. If I don't get a scoop, what's gonna happen to my kid? He's blind as a bat. You know what it's like to live in a world where you can't tell one color from another? (*As if suddenly coming to, notices the* SOLDIER's *hands on the* GIRL's *breast. Dryly*) Will you cut that out? Will you? (*Goes back to his writing*) Now you think they got a half-dozen guys on the upper-echelon levels dividing them up?

SOLDIER

Dividing what up?

HARRY

The colors! (SOLDIER *shrugs*) Okay. I'm quoting you. Would it surprise you if I knew who some of these men are?

SOLDIER

No, man.

HARRY

You see that guy picking his nose?
(SOLDIER *turns around and looks offstage*)

SOLDIER

Who? The guy with the beret?

HARRY

Not the guy with the beret. The guy picking his nose.

SOLDIER

He's got a red scarf?

[ 175 ]

HARRY

Not the red scarf. The guy picking his nose.

SOLDIER

I don't see anybody picking his nose.

HARRY

(*Violently, and rising out of his seat to point*)
Him! Him!

SOLDIER

(*Staring as hard as he can*)
Yeah. He's leaning up against the jukebox, right?

HARRY

That's the guy who was doing the dirty boogy. I'm talking about the one picking his nose.

SOLDIER

Yeah. I see him now. It's the smoke in here. What about him?

HARRY

You sure you see him?

SOLDIER

Yeah, I see him now. What about him?

HARRY

He's one of the guys who decides about the division of color. (SOLDIER *looks at* HARRY *disbelievingly*) He's in the Color Division Section.

[ 176 ]

SOLDIER

Man, I don't . . .

HARRY

See the way he's rubbing his hand up and down that soldier's back. Wattya think he's doing that for? He's checking on the color temperature of his uniform. Every color's got a different heat level.

SOLDIER

(*Staring off real hard*)

Is he picking his nose, now? The smoke in here is fierce.

HARRY

(*Violently. Twists the* SOLDIER's *head in the direction he wants him to look*)

Him! Over there. Goddam it, what the hell's wrong with you. Him! Now he's patting his little brother on the head. The kid with the cigarette.

SOLDIER

There's no kids allowed in here.

HARRY

Pretty soon he'll whop the kid for smoking. That's the way he operates. Move in close, smiling, and then, whop with his snotty hands. (*Pause while they stare offstage.* GIRL *starts waving at other customers*) Whop! (*Shouts*) That's a way to go. That's a way. Don't give anyone a chance! (*To* SOLDIER) Ask him to join us.

SOLDIER

What for?

HARRY

So we can find out once and for all why things are divided up the way they are.

SOLDIER

Man, she's gonna leave me.

HARRY

No she won't.

SOLDIER
(*Striking down her hands*)

Don't wave.

HARRY
(*Grabs the front of her blouse*)

I'll hold her.

SOLDIER

I can't just walk up to the guy and ask him to come over.

HARRY

Sure you can.

SOLDIER
(*Confidentially*)

It's what the queers do.

HARRY

And find out what the kid is doing in here smoking a cigarette. Did you ever see such an evil-looking little bastard? Look at him. Wouldn't you like to whop him too?

[ 178 ]

SOLDIER

They don't allow kids in here. Maybe it's a midget.

HARRY

Well, for Christ's sake, find out.

SOLDIER

Man, why don't you find out?

HARRY

On account of my lungs. I can't get into places where they got too much smoke.

SOLDIER

(*Unwillingly gets up*)

You hold onto her good.

HARRY

I got her by the leg and breast.

SOLDIER

Don't go away, baby.

HARRY

I got her. Watch out for his snotty hands. (SOLDIER *walks off-stage.* HARRY *shouts after*) Keep outta range of the nose. (*The* SOLDIER *is evidently looking back because* HARRY *keeps waving directions with his arms. While* HARRY *is violently engaged in giving directions, he talks. The* GIRL *begins working him over*) That's what I should've been. A strafer. Get everything in a burst. Right through the heart. Watch things crumble up under

[ 179 ]

my guns. Piece by piece, like powder. Get 'em even in the hospitals. Hide in the corner, I crumble up the wall. Piece by piece. Let 'em have it with a fifty right in the ladies' room. Crumble up like powder. No hiding place. (*Rising from chair, shouts to* SOLDIER) Not the guy doing the dirty boogy. The nosepicker. Him! Him! (*Violently slaps* GIRL. *She falls to floor, as he utters a cry of anguish. Turns in direction of* SOLDIER, *wildly shouting and gesturing*) Him! Him!

**CURTAIN**

# Scene Two

*Immanuel entertains a visitor from Ohio*

PLACE: HARRY *and* IMMANUEL'*s room.*

TIME: *The same afternoon.*

SCENE: *The room is a combination kitchen, bedroom, living room and studio. The kitchen area — sink, shelves, cupboards, coal stove — is on the left side of the room. On the upstage side of the kitchen is a toilet, a small partitioned cubicle jutting into the room. It is the old pull-chain type toilet and the water box is clearly visible above the partition. The door is open. Somewhat below and right of center is a bed, with the headpost facing and a few feet away from the right wall. Near the foot of the bed is a small walking-cane chair of 1939 World's Fair vintage. A table, littered with assorted articles, separates the cane-chair from a comfortable upholstered chair. Downstage right wall has a curtained window. Various paintings, finished and unfinished, are strewn around the room, particularly along the right wall. On the upstage wall, in line with the bed, is a dresser. Between the bed and dresser, on the right wall, is a stand-up closet. A clothesline stretches from the wall on the upstage side of the bed to the upstage wall on the right side of the dresser. In the general vicinity is an open ironing board. A metal stand holding several potted plants is on the left side of the dresser. The entrance door is upstage, left of center. Near the entrance is a phonograph; the lid is open.*

ON RISE: IMMANUEL, *an ascetic-looking individual in his middle twenties, is cleaning a fish on a small table, down-stage left. He cleans with a great deal of precision and a definite degree of relish. The feeling we get is that this fish is more than a fish, perhaps an old enemy being disposed of.* IMMANUEL *keeps mumbling to himself in German. Occasionally, a single word or phrase becomes audible. The mumbling is directed toward the fish. The audible words are such as: bones, blood, head, scales.*

IMMANUEL'*s movements are quick, nervous, insectile. He is wearing an old robe with a shedding fur collar that might be cat fur.*

ARCHER, *a big heavy-set person approaching his forties, wearing an expensive-looking topcoat, carrying a rolled-up copy of the* Saturday Evening Post, *is poking around the room examining the contents. He has the involuntary habit of scratching at his nose, and in the general vicinity of his nose.*

ARCHER

As a matter of fact, Harry forgot to mention that the street sign is just a twisted pole. It looks like somebody sheared the top of it right off. And the one on the other end of the street looks like it was hit by a Mack truck loaded with India ink. You couldn't read it if your life depended on it.

IMMANUEL

This is Andvari Strasse.

ARCHER

That's not the point. The point is that whoever is in charge
of keeping those signs in good repair is falling down on his job.
What you people on this block ought to do is complain to the
City Street Commission. Get them to send someone down here
and fix up what should be fixed up.

IMMANUEL

Some things will not be fixed.

ARCHER

Everything can be fixed but you have to have the right attitude. You can't just give up about it. I'll tell you something else
that's mighty sad about this street. There isn't a house on the
entire block with a number on it. Next time you're out take a
look. Wait a minute. I take that back. There was one house
with a number on it and some kid with a dachshund was digging out the number plate with a screwdriver.

IMMANUEL

This is seventy-four.

ARCHER
( *Starts searching his pockets* )
Wait a minute. I got the number my brother gave me.
( *Searches a few seconds more and then finds it. Looks at it
to confirm the wrong address* ) This is what he wrote.
       ( *Hands it to* IMMANUEL. IMMANUEL *more or less pulls it
       out of his hands and stares at it* )

IMMANUEL

Seventy-two.
       ( *Stiffly hands* ARCHER *the fishy slip of paper.* ARCHER *with*

[ 183 ]

*some trepidation takes it. He looks around for a place to dispose of it* )

ARCHER

You have a garbage pail or something? (IMMANUEL *lets the question hang in the air just a second or so more than is necessary, to create a feeling of imposition. Then he holds out his hand.* ARCHER *puts the paper in his hand.* IMMANUEL *goes to the hall door.* IMMANUEL *limps on his left foot. He opens the door and throws the paper out in the hall. He turns and comes back limping on his right foot.* ARCHER *doesn't seem to notice that the limp has switched feet. All* IMMANUEL's *walking will be done this way* ) If it wasn't for an old lady walking a Pomeranian I'd still be marching up and down the street. How Harry can write down seventy-two when he lives at seventy-four I'll never know. Wait, I take that back. (*He gives an irritating little laugh* ) The summer he flunked his pre-flight physical he decided to come into the family business and help the accountant. You know what he did? He confused the figures in the purchase and sales ledgers and debited where he should have credited and credited where he should have debited. He just could not get it right.

IMMANUEL

You have yesterday's address.

ARCHER

What?

IMMANUEL

Today we are seventy-four because the building that was seventy-four when we were seventy-two fell down. If the building next door falls down we advance to seventy-six. If we fall down, they advance to seventy-eight. Last month we were sixty-eight. (IMMANUEL *becomes particularly vicious toward the fish*) Only sixty-eight. Soon we will be the highest number on the street!

(*Said with the gusto usually reserved for such statements as "Today Europe; Tomorrow the World"*)

ARCHER
(*Holding his stomach*)
Oh, damn. Stomach's been sour as hell since I got off the train. If the public health people did their job inspecting the fruit that's peddled around . . . Look, excuse me a second, will you. (*Puts magazine on table, takes off his overcoat and suit jacket and heads for the small toilet. Once inside, he tries to shut the door. The door keeps swinging open*) What's wrong with this door?

IMMANUEL
It keeps opening.

ARCHER
Yeah, I know it keeps opening. What you need is a lock so you can get some privacy. You don't wanna have to sit here with your foot hooked under it.

IMMANUEL
It can't be fixed.

ARCHER
Of course it can be fixed. All you need's a latch. Anybody can put a latch on. (ARCHER *comes out and begins dressing again as he makes his speech. He is extremely fastidious*) What I

don't understand is why Harry left the art school in Florence
four months ago without notifying the family. People in close-
knit families don't do things like that. The girls, Harry's sisters,
were sending food packages to Florence and somebody down
there all the months Harry's been wandering around Munich
was signing his name and eating his food. I don't expect American postal standards from the Italians, I remember the Italians
from the war when they were stealing your eyeteeth, but there
are some standards that have to be maintained. Improper handling of the mail is a federal offense, it just is that. If a Lion
friend of mine . . . that's a business fraternity . . . didn't
have a son stationed in Munich who accidentally ran into Harry
in a museum we'd still be sending food packages to the thief
in Florence. When Harry found out the school was no good —
and that's the general trouble with Europe, it's overrated — he
should have written me and I would'a started hunting him up
a good school in America. The kid knows the family's behind
him all the way, right to the goalpost. The better the mind you
got the longer it takes to find yourself. A lot of people like
Harry don't find themselves until they're in their thirties. Then,
all of a sudden, they turn out OK. Harry'll make it OK. But you
just don't run out of Florence, drop down in the middle of nowhere and vanish. You just don't do that when you belong to a
family. The Bible'll tell you that . . . no man is an island all
by himself. All Harry needs is a good art school in America. A
fresh start again. There's nothing wrong with Ohio State. Some
damn fine Americans came out of Ohio State.

IMMANUEL

(*Gestures with an air of surprise toward the toilet*)
You are finished?

[ 186 ]

ARCHER

I'll wait till I get to the restaurant.

IMMANUEL

It is not good to wait.

ARCHER

I'm all right. Did Harry say when he'd be back?

IMMANUEL

To suffer is not good.

ARCHER

I'm all right! Let's just drop it. You said he was at the museum before. Do you know when it closes? (IMMANUEL *starts mumbling in German to the fish. He wildly scrapes the scales*) What?

IMMANUEL
(*Mumbles*)

It is not good to wait. (*Feverishly*) Soon. Soon. He's at the museum. All have different closing times. One closes one hour, another closes another hour, another closes later, another closes . . .

ARCHER

What's the matter here? I just . . .
(IMMANUEL *continues as if* ARCHER *had said nothing*)

IMMANUEL

. . . another hour. Some of them close at three, some at four, two of them at five, one stays open to nine. (*And then, emphatically, as if it really matters*) To nine!

ARCHER

What the point here is, is that I made reservations for Harry and me to eat at the Hermitage at five. (*Looks at his watch*) And that's what it almost is now. I don't want to have to eat that train food and neither does Harry. Look, do you have a phone? I'd better move up the reservations.

IMMANUEL

This fish is for Harry and me. There isn't enough for others.

ARCHER
(*Still looking for the phone*)

You're missing the point. Harry and I are going out to eat. What you wanna do is get this room shaped up. I can't seem to find the phone.

IMMANUEL

We always eat in. It isn't fair changing the eating arrangements without notice. It's a small fish.
(*Holds the fish up. The fish is quite large*)

ARCHER

Where's the phone?

IMMANUEL

(*Looks around as if searching for a phone.* ARCHER *impatiently waits.* IMMANUEL *reaches behind him into a cupboard, presumably reaching for the phone. He pulls out a salt shaker and furiously shakes it over the fish*)
There is no phone.

ARCHER

Oh, this is something to write home about.

[ 188 ]

IMMANUEL

Harry made me take it out. He doesn't want me calling my
friends. He's got it in for them.

ARCHER

(*Stares at him for a second. Seems about to say some-
thing, but doesn't*)
Okay, you just clean the fish.
(*Goes over to the comfortable chair*)

IMMANUEL

That's Harry's chair. Nobody sits in Harry's chair.

ARCHER

I'm sure Harry won't mind. I've come four thousand miles to
escort him home, so he won't mind if I rest in his chair. (*Sits
down and is greeted by a rising cloud of talcum powder*) What
the hell! (*He stands up and begins brushing off the back of his
trousers*) There's powder all over my pants! Jesus Christ. What
is this? Some kind of joke?

IMMANUEL

Harry doesn't want Juju and Michael sitting in his chair.

ARCHER

(*Hits the cushion and a cloud of talcum powder rises*)
My God.

IMMANUEL

Juju and Michael always want to sit in Harry's chair.

[ 189 ]

ARCHER

( *Now trying to pound the powder out of his pants* )
Boy, this is great, just great. Harry did this? Oh, this isn't
going to come out.

IMMANUEL

I have fluid that will cleanse a stain.
( *Starts searching in the cupboard* )

ARCHER

Hurry up. Jesus H. Christ! I don't understand this. How do
you go about putting powder in chairs? What kind of a thing
is that? ( IMMANUEL *comes limping out pouring the cleaning
fluid in a sponge. He starts wiping the back of the pants with
it* ) Christ, it's on the jacket, too. ( *Takes off his jacket* ) Is it
coming off? What kind of cleaning fluid is that?

IMMANUEL

It will cleanse a stain. Take off your pants.

ARCHER

Can't you get it?

IMMANUEL

You must take off your pants.
( *There is a pause.* ARCHER *is dubious about taking his
pants off. He gives* IMMANUEL *the jacket* )

ARCHER

Get some of that fluid on the jacket. ( IMMANUEL *rubs the
cleaning fluid on the jacket while* ARCHER *begins taking his*

*pants off.* IMMANUEL *brings the pants over to the ironing board
and rubs furiously, with* ARCHER *hovering over him*) Some of
those newer cleaning fluids work like magic.

IMMANUEL

(*Supposedly annoyed because* ARCHER *is hovering over
him*)
Please. (*And then loudly and angrily*) Please!
(ARCHER *goes back and sits on the little cane-chair.* IM-
MANUEL *rubs and rubs*)

ARCHER

Watch the nap. You can't rub it too hard. What kind of cleaning fluid is that?

IMMANUEL

Please! (*He hangs the suit up on the line. The pants should
be hung so that the audience can see that the stain is not going
to come out*) Now they must dry. (*From across the street the
bells of the convent start tolling the hour. They toll five times*)
The sacred bells from the convent of Our Sisters of Healing,
Grace and Forgiveness.

ARCHER

Fine.

IMMANUEL

They ring every fifteen minutes.

ARCHER

Fine.

IMMANUEL

(*Goes over to a dresser and pulls out a selection of beads and crucifixes. He brings them over*)

You are interested in things of religion? Perhaps a purchase? Here it is possible to make a fantastic purchase. (*Displays them*) Beads? Crucifixes?

ARCHER

No. I don't think . . . (IMMANUEL *begins waving them in front of his face*) Must you wave them in front of my face?

IMMANUEL

This is a fantastic purchase for you. Harry doesn't know I have things of religion.

(*Still waving them*)

ARCHER

I'll bet he doesn't. How much are they? Get them out of my face.

IMMANUEL

All prices.

ARCHER

(*Picking up a string of beads*)

How much are these?

IMMANUEL

Fifty cents American money.

ARCHER

(*Pointing to another set of identical beads*)

And these?

IMMANUEL

Nine dollars American money.


ARCHER

(*Takes them both in his hands and studies them*)
I can't see any difference.


IMMANUEL

There is a difference. (ARCHER *looks at them more closely*)
Can't you see the difference?
(IMMANUEL *begins squinting at them as well*)


ARCHER

They look the same to me.


IMMANUEL

(*Grabs them out of his hand and squints at them by himself*)
There is a difference. A difference.
(*He starts to put them away in the dresser*)


ARCHER

Never mind. I'll take the fifty-cent beads.
(*But* IMMANUEL *puts them back in the dresser as if he didn't hear* ARCHER *speak*)


IMMANUEL

I have some holy water.


ARCHER

Don't bother. I'll take the beads.

[ 193 ]

IMMANUEL

Harry only wishes he possessed holy water. (*He goes over to the refrigerator and pulls out a milk bottle full of water and carefully pours some of it into a little stoppered flask. He returns with the flask*) Fresh because you are Harry's brother. You perhaps noticed that the holy water was kept in an ordinary milk bottle. That is done to confound thieves. Do not be deluded by appearances. (*Holds out bottle*) Smell it. (ARCHER *is hesitant*) Just smell it. Smell it! (ARCHER *smells it*) What does it smell like? Egypt? Babylon? Syria?

ARCHER

It smells like water. I can't smell anything.

IMMANUEL

(*Grabs it out of his hands and smells it himself*)
There is a difference. A difference. (*Limps off with it to the refrigerator where he carefully begins pouring it back into the milk bottle. He faces* ARCHER) You are the only one who does not smell the difference! (*Before* ARCHER *has a chance to reply he turns back to the refrigerator and finishes pouring the liquid back*) There is a difference. The sisters of the convent assured me. There were assurances made.

ARCHER

What do you do, buy your stuff at the convent?

IMMANUEL

(*Slams refrigerator door and turns around*)
Relics? I had some bones, knee and thigh and finger bones in good condition . . . but there were dogs . . . aaagh! (*Falls*

*down on his knees and starts searching under the bed*) Harry
doesn't know I have bone relics. He would envy me.

ARCHER

Look . . . Harry wouldn't know a bone relic from a church
door. I don't know what he's been telling you but . . .

IMMANUEL

(*With* IMMANUEL *under the bed,* ARCHER *has a chance to
pick his nose in private*)
What I possess here is special. Special! You are familiar with
the beautiful Christian virgin, St. Juliana? Eh? Eh?

ARCHER

No.

IMMANUEL

Beautiful virgin, beautiful thighs. Aagh. Her father gave her
to a pagan for his bride, but she would not marry a pagan. She
must renounce Christ. They threatened her with torture. She
tried to flee but it was no use . . . her beautiful thighs were not
fast enough . . . beautiful thighs. Aagh. They hung her upside down and beat her. Scourged by whips, the blood ran up
the soft flesh of her thighs. Aaagh. They said to keep the holy
nail clippings in the dark, and that if I put them in the sun they
would grow. There was much blood. The more she refused her
cruel father's wishes, the more they caressed her thighs with
whips. Into a vat of boiling lead. Then the chopping. There
were nail clippings taken from her fingers and toes. Thighs.
Aagh. White thighs. Yes. Clippings taken. (IMMANUEL *pokes
his head suddenly out from under the bed.* ARCHER *is caught*

*with his finger in his nose.* IMMANUEL *looks at him for a second.*
ARCHER's *hand drops*) Nail clippings? (*He comes forward.
Somehow the limp in his leg has turned into a walk that is
overtly feminine and suggestive*) Nail clippings? (*Thrusts an
ashtray filled with nail clippings under* ARCHER's *nose*) You are
interested in the nail clippings of saints?

(*Here we must believe that there is a sort of hypnosis
going on, effected both by* IMMANUEL's *sexual movements
and also by a kind of eye contact*)

ARCHER

No. (*And then slower, as if apologetic*) Not at all. Really.

IMMANUEL

Harry would envy you. Relics like these are unobtainable
elsewhere. If you do not purchase here . . . Do you wish to
touch them?

ARCHER

No. Not . . . I don't wish to touch them.

IMMANUEL

Touch them. Do not torment yourself. I can see you long to
touch them.

ARCHER

I don't long to touch them. I wouldn't touch those filthy . . .

IMMANUEL

You wish to touch them only you are ashamed. You imagine
there will be laughter, that you will seem foolish. I will not
laugh at your heart's desire. Here you may do as you please.

[ 196 ]

ARCHER
(*Feebly*)

I'm not ashamed.

IMMANUEL

Don't be ashamed.

ARCHER

I don't . . .

IMMANUEL
(*Suddenly and authoritatively*)

Touch them! (ARCHER *almost instinctively reaches out and
sticks his hand in the ashtray*) You feel better now. Here there
is nothing to be ashamed of. (*And then, almost casually, as*
IMMANUEL *turns from him*) You ought to use a mouthwash. No
matter. No matter.

(*This jolts* ARCHER *out of whatever state he was in*)

ARCHER

What did you say?

IMMANUEL
(*Puts the ashtray on the nightstand, picks up a black
glove and starts putting it on*)

Do you mind if I wear my medical glove?

ARCHER

What did you say about the mouthwash?

IMMANUEL

There are some who mind the medical glove. Do you mind?

[ 197 ]

ARCHER

No.

IMMANUEL

I have a skin condition. Perhaps you noticed?

ARCHER

No.

IMMANUEL

That is kind of you. When I was born there were certain handicaps . . . but it is boring for Americans to listen to recitals of infirmities. You would like to see Harry's American art while you are waiting? So. (*Escorts* ARCHER *by the arm over to the paintings.* ARCHER *doesn't enjoy being touched*) To have bad breath is not the worst calamity. You have never had eczema, of course.

ARCHER

No.

IMMANUEL

Impetigo? Seborrheic dermatitis? Acne vulgaris? Ringworm?

ARCHER

Look, I don't want to be rude . . . I've always been well. (*Looks at* HARRY'S *paintings*) Harry was doing more representational things in Ohio. Portraits. Landscapes. He did one of sailboats in a harbor that the whole family liked. (*Holds one out from him. The painting is a garish blotch of discordant color*) What's this one represent?

[ 198 ]

IMMANUEL

Hunchbacks eating strawberries. They are looking at the thighs of a young girl. She is sweet, clean. As a child, my skin became greasy and I noticed small holes appearing in the skin. I washed and washed with soaps and salts but there was dirt I could not wash out.

ARCHER

Wait a minute.
*(He puts the canvas down and steps back a few feet)*

IMMANUEL

Do you see their half-shut dreamy eyes contemplating what must not even be thought? The slow movements of the child's naked shoulders inviting their languid blue eyes.

ARCHER

I can't make it out. I don't see any child.

IMMANUEL

You see? You see? The thighs . . . I was meticulous in cleanliness, but the disease lay dormant for months and years. Foulodored sweat that perfume could not conceal nor baths of potassium permanganate dispel. I rubbed the clefts of my toes, but plugs of dirt were already forming in the skin . . . She will break their hearts. Their hearts will not be mended. She is without pity.

ARCHER
*(Still staring at the painting)*
I can't make this out. Where is the child?

[ 199 ]

IMMANUEL

(*Violently pointing*)

There is the child!


ARCHER

(*Pointing doubtfully*)

And those are the hunchbacks?


IMMANUEL

Yes. Yes. They are suffering. They long for what they may not have. She taunts them. She teases them. She leads them on. She is without mercy.


ARCHER

I can't . . . Which is the girl again?


IMMANUEL

(*This time he runs over to the painting and shoves his finger against it*)

This! This! Look how wicked she is with her innocence. She thinks because she is innocent she can break their hearts. She thinks they are foul toads; that there is no limit to the warts that may be thrust upon them. There is a limit to the number of warts! It is not enough for her that their backs are bent under the sun and under her yoke. That . . . (*Points again*) is all she thinks she must do . . . smile . . . but she does not smile . . . she is lewd . . . she leers. You like this?


ARCHER

When Harry gets back to Ohio, he'll get in the swing again. What's under the towel?

[ 200 ]

IMMANUEL

I do not understand. Swing? This is wonderful art, for any house. Matches all colors.

ARCHER

This . . . (*Goes over and picks up his magazine, the* Saturday Evening Post. *Shows it to* IMMANUEL) . . . this is art. Norman Rockwell. Ever hear of Norman Rockwell? If Harry'd get on the stick he could paint rings around him.

IMMANUEL

What are they doing?

ARCHER

Whatta ya mean, what are they doing? They're eating a turkey. It's Thanksgiving.

IMMANUEL
(*Pointing*)

What's that?

ARCHER

That's the turkey. You better get yourself a pair of glasses. Skip it. What's under the towel? (IMMANUEL *pulls the cloth off the* Stone-blind Kid, *a small Victorian cupidlike statue without eyes*) That's more like it. That's good. This has got it. I've seen lots of homes with these cupids. What's the matter with its eyes?

IMMANUEL

It's blind.

ARCHER

It's unfinished, that's all. You don't make blind statues. He hasn't even put the fig leaf over the . . . the organ.

IMMANUEL

It's finished. You wish to buy? You have plaster deer on your lawn? Stone water fountains? This could be ideally placed near a stone water fountain. Harry says American lawns have blue mirrored balls. This could be placed near such a ball.

ARCHER

If Harry wants to give it to me, he'll give it. I don't buy from Harry.

IMMANUEL

You buy from me! It is mine. I buy all Harry's work. Notice the upraised supplicating arms. Useful to hold magazines in bathrooms. *Saturday Evening Post, Ladies' Home Journal, Reader's Digest.* You read in bathrooms?

ARCHER

That's none of your . . . No. I don't read in bathrooms.
        (*He has been scratching his nose*)

IMMANUEL

Harry reads in the bathroom. (*He begins scratching the glove*) When the skin is hypersensitive the slightest little irritant that would be entirely harmless upon healthy skin erupts and must be scratched and once scratched the itch grows and grows in an inflammatory temptation that cannot be resisted. A demon. (*Suddenly he switches from scratching the glove to*

[ 202 ]

*scratching his nose.* ARCHER *immediately drops his hand to his side*) No matter. No matter. (IMMANUEL *goes over to the bed, removes* ARCHER's *topcoat, places it across the back of the up-holstered chair, and then sits down on the bed.* ARCHER, *slightly taken aback by* HARRY's *art work, walks backward a few feet still looking at it. He finally sits in the small cane-chair. He is obviously thinking*) You do not mind if I sit?

ARCHER

What?

IMMANUEL

You do not mind if I sit?

ARCHER
(*Waves his arm*)
Why should I mind if you sit?

IMMANUEL

At present I am contemplating a book attacking Hegel's dialectic. (*He removes a slipper from his foot*) Will you hand me the scissors?
(*The scissors rest on a small table in between the cane-chair and* HARRY's *chair. Motions to the scissors.* ARCHER *brings them over*)

ARCHER

He used to paint the damnedest harbor scenes.
(*Hands scissors to* IMMANUEL)

IMMANUEL

Good of you. You are familiar with Hegel's dialectic?

ARCHER

What?

IMMANUEL

Do you regard the absolute as pure being, as nothing, or as the union of being and not being?

ARCHER

I don't regard it as anything. I'm not much for philosophy. I'm just a businessman.

IMMANUEL

Most *businessmen* are not aware that Hegel studied under Thomas Aquinas. That's where Hegel's error comes from. There is no unmoved mover. There is only the moved moving.

ARCHER

I told you I wasn't much for philosophy.

IMMANUEL

No matter. No matter. Consider the case of an arrow in flight. In terms of existence what is it that exists, the arrow or the flight?

ARCHER

I'm just not getting through to you.

IMMANUEL

Or consider the question of self. What is the self that it should be hounded and not left to die? To be left to die, a dark corner to scratch all the itches. To scratch.

[ 204 ]

ARCHER

How long have you and Harry been living together?

IMMANUEL

What is time? Illusion. What is illusion? What we will. The perfume, please. (ARCHER *reaches out to the same table and gets the perfume. He brings it over.* IMMANUEL *dabs his feet with the perfume*) Would you like me to wash your feet in perfume?

ARCHER

For God's sake! I'm all right. Are you sure Harry's at the museum?

IMMANUEL

Yes. Every afternoon he goes to the museum, but he will be here any moment now. Harry and I find the perfume relaxing to the legs.

ARCHER

I thought you didn't know when he was coming back.

IMMANUEL

I assure you, any moment. Will you hand me my cigarettes?

ARCHER

Where are . . . (*They are on the same table everything else was on. He silently brings them over*) If you put that table over here you'd be organized. (*Meaning the table* ARCHER's *been fetching from*) The both of you could use a little of that. (IMMANUEL *lights his cigarette and inhales*

*deeply. He puts the cigarette down and sticking the leg fully*
*out of the bathrobe proceeds to rub the perfume on*) You both
sleep in this bed?

IMMANUEL

Yes. It is our bed. Do you wish to relax till Harry gets here?

ARCHER

I'm comfortable here.

IMMANUEL

Do not feel embarrassed. I can see you're tired and wish to
relax. Your spine must be paining you on that little chair.
Come. Lie down, here.
(*Patting the bed*)

ARCHER

I'm fine.

IMMANUEL

No matter. No matter. (*He reaches into the night table*
*drawer and pulls out a woman's nylon stocking. He begins*
*massaging his leg and putting the stocking on.* ARCHER *is re-*
*vulsed, tries to look away*) The cold dilates the blood vessels
in my leg. Special precautions must be taken. You can see the
leg is weak. Hair cannot seem to grow on it. Therefore I must
keep it warm. Perhaps you are familiar with legs like mine?
Doctors have been unable to help. I go to bed early in the
evening when the blood is most active. Then I sleep. The leg
is warm. The thigh is hot. I am delirious with happiness. While
I sleep, the snow falls layer upon layer, the chill advances

[ 206 ]

through the window, under the door. It comes under the bed and touches my leg. I ignore it, but the pain grows. I will not have anything to do with it. Out. Out. But the pain stabs at the heel, at the arch. It cannot be ignored. It lowers the temperature in my calf, it chills the thigh. My leg is now encased in ice. The pain is exquisite. The ligaments are torn at, they stretch, they twist, they tighten into the bones, I am in torture. I cannot bear to be touched. I throw the bedclothes from me. I move from this side to that side, but it is worse. The pain heightens; it grows more exquisite, fits of terror overtake my thigh. There is no respite from the pain. No movement that will free the leg. I twist; I turn; my leg is encased in icy pain; there is no fleeing, no remedy, I die . . . but the night passes, the sun comes, I throw my leg in the sun, the yellow heat flames upon the calf, the thigh . . .

ARCHER

Well, I'm going to wait at the restaurant. (*Gets up and goes over to the clothesline to feel the stain on his pants*) It still isn't dry! What did you put on it?

IMMANUEL

It will be cleansed. Do not keep touching it, and handling it, and fondling it.

ARCHER

Then why is it still wet? I don't understand that. Any cleaning fluid should be dry by now.

IMMANUEL

You do not mind if I stretch out further?

[ 207 ]

ARCHER

Why should I mind? Why should . . . (*He holds his stomach, and winces*) Goddam it.

IMMANUEL

You wish to use my toilet?

ARCHER

I'm all right.

IMMANUEL

It is there for your use.

ARCHER

(*Recovers*)

The pants should be dry in another minute or two, then I'm leaving. You can tell Harry to meet me at the Hermitage!

IMMANUEL

No matter. No matter. (*He begins cavorting under the covers. He turns and twists, in a rather sexual manner*) My spine is damaged. Perhaps you noticed? That is why I must twist about.

ARCHER

I didn't notice.

IMMANUEL

Ah, kind of you to say so.

ARCHER

I didn't notice!

[ 208 ]

IMMANUEL

You did not notice the stoop?

ARCHER

No. I told you I don't notice things like that.

IMMANUEL

With most people it is the first thing they notice, but I have become philosophical about it. Once in the park I was set upon by children. Several stones were thrown. I chased the children but they ran and my leg is twisted.

(*Dangles leg out of the bed and then coquettishly withdraws it*)

ARCHER

It looks all right.

IMMANUEL

No matter. No matter. It is of no importance. I accept. It is for that reason I must stretch the length of my spine against the mattress. You understand? It is all right?

ARCHER

Please! Do as you like!

IMMANUEL

(*Crawling further under the covers*)

I will just pull the coverlet up to my neck, no higher. I find that unless my neck is warm my shoulders ache. (*Managing to thrust a shoulder out and then withdrawing it.* ARCHER, *uncomfortable on the cane-chair, has moved over to the side of* HARRY's *chair. He sits down on the arm.* IMMANUEL *begins patting the bed*) Come, you are tired. Sit beside me on the bed and we will talk.

ARCHER

I'll be leaving in a minute.

IMMANUEL

Why weary your back? Why torment your spine . . . If only for a minute . . . You must be tired. There is no need for formality. Come, stretch yourself beside me. It is too cold not to be together. Come. Come.

ARCHER

I don't understand why it takes those pants so long to dry. Can I see Harry coming from this window?

IMMANUEL

No matter. Yes. You can see all the way down the street from that window. ( ARCHER *walks over to the window*) Do not touch the curtains! Please!

ARCHER

I only wanted to pull . . .

IMMANUEL

The window faces a convent. The curtains are never pulled.

ARCHER

I just wanted to look out in the street.

IMMANUEL

It is a matter of religious principle, the Catholic mysteries.

[ 210 ]

ARCHER

I can't see what religion has to do . . .

IMMANUEL

I have made a Catholic vow. You mustn't tell Harry I'm a Catholic.

ARCHER

I'm not going to say anything.

IMMANUEL

Harry doesn't know anything about the beads. I tell him they are for children. I pretend the holy water is ice water. I don't want him to know. You won't say anything?

ARCHER

I'm not going to say anything.

IMMANUEL

I pretend the nail clippings are from my feet. He thinks I'm an orthodox Jew. I was forced to buy a yomulka and go to synagogue on Fridays because Harry wanted to see, but then on Sunday I took in an early-morning Mass.

ARCHER

Look, I don't care about your religion. That's the American way. If you wanna sit on a flagpole bowing to Mecca that's your business.

IMMANUEL

I confessed on Sunday. The priest said it would be all right if I confessed on Sundays. Do you think that makes it all right — if I do evil and then confess on Sunday?

[ 211 ]

ARCHER

If the priest said it was all right, it's all right.


IMMANUEL

Yes. Of course. But if the priest made a mistake, then I'm doomed. It's a matter of grave importance. (ARCHER *has wandered close to the bed*) Come, give me your hand. (*Seizes* ARCHER's *hand*) Come, come. (*Pulls* ARCHER *down on the bed beside him. As he mentions each part of his body he puts* ARCHER's *hand on the part.* ARCHER *is increasingly repelled*) Feel my hands. Like ice. That may be a sign. A foreshadowing. I don't want to wait till the eleventh hour. If the priest made a mistake, I'm doomed. (*His hopes pick up*) But my throat is warm. Feel my throat. It's warm. Do my shoulders seem hot or cold to you. The left is warmer than the right, is that not so? That is a good sign. (*Hopes fade*) But here, here, the heart is cold. Feel my back. The hump is hot. Feel my hump.


ARCHER

(*Manages to pull his hand free*)
Get hold of yourself. What's wrong with you?


IMMANUEL

It is a matter of grave importance.


ARCHER

Priests are infallible. If he told you it's all right, it's all right.


IMMANUEL

Only the Pope is infallible. That's what tortures me. Priests can make mistakes. Hell is full of priestly mistakes. The soul in hell melts like a wax candle, the blood dries to red powder, the eyes burst and flow like jelly down the cheek.

(IMMANUEL *is all upset.* ARCHER *puts his arms around* IMMANUEL *and comforts him. Rocks* IMMANUEL *like a baby*)

#### ARCHER

It's all right. All right.

(*Suddenly* IMMANUEL *recovers, lies back and smiles at* ARCHER)

#### IMMANUEL

I feel better now. That is why I'm writing this book attacking Thomas Aquinas.

#### ARCHER

(*Gets up and pulls his pants off the clothesline. He begins dressing*)

Listen, you were just writing on Segel or somebody.

#### IMMANUEL

You're mistaken. You do not see things as they are. I am revising. I cannot continue with Segel. My father wants me to continue with Segel but I cannot.

#### ARCHER

(*Has the pants on, but he sees they are too wet*)

Jesus. It's getting through to my underwear. (*He goes over to the stove and keeps his back to it*) What kind of cleaning fluid doesn't dry? Jesus Christ.

#### IMMANUEL

Perhaps you saw him selling balloons at the corner?

[ 213 ]

ARCHER

(*Not paying any attention*)

If these pants are ruined . . .

IMMANUEL

(*Shouting*)

Perhaps you saw my father selling balloons!

ARCHER

No. All right? All right?

(*From below somebody has been disturbed by the yelling and knocks up.* IMMANUEL *reaches out and grabs a
thick wooden cane. He pounds the cane on the floor until
the pounding below ceases. And then, as if there had been
no interruption*)

IMMANUEL

He keeps a vicious red monkey to attract the children.

ARCHER

I didn't see him.

IMMANUEL

He's at the corner every day.

ARCHER

I didn't see him . . . all right?

IMMANUEL

Once a week he lets a single balloon loose. The string slips
through his fingers. The balloon rises over the roofs and then
lunges for the moon.

ARCHER

(*Looking at his pants*)

Jesus.

IMMANUEL

You didn't . . .

ARCHER

No!

IMMANUEL

He wears a red jacket. Will you look?

ARCHER

What?

IMMANUEL

Will you look and see if he's there? He wears a red jacket.

ARCHER

I thought you didn't want me to look out the window!

IMMANUEL

Yes, you may look. If you look just to the right. The convent is to the left.

ARCHER

I tell you he isn't there. I would have seen him when . . .

IMMANUEL

Will you look? Please! (ARCHER *goes over to the window*) Just move the curtain back a little. You will not look at the convent?

[ 215 ]

ARCHER

I'm not going to look at the convent. Why should I want to look at the convent?

IMMANUEL

Sometimes he takes a little child in back of the convent. You have only to move the curtain back a hairsbreadth to see him.

ARCHER

All right. All right.

IMMANUEL

Only a hairsbreadth. Slowly, slowly. There are mysteries. Do not move it too much. He goes in back of the altar of the convent where the nuns never come. He thinks he will be safe there. (*Sharply*) Do not look to the left.

ARCHER

I'm not looking to the left.

IMMANUEL

Please do not look to the left.

ARCHER

There's nobody there.

IMMANUEL

He is wearing a red jacket. He always wears a red jacket. He's always there.

ARCHER

Well, maybe he left. All right?

IMMANUEL

You're looking to the left.

ARCHER

I'm looking to the right. All they got out there is two nuns waiting for a trolley.

IMMANUEL

Are they moonfaced? Sometimes it is a matter of disguise.

ARCHER

Just two nuns! . . . Which way does Harry come?

IMMANUEL

From the left. Don't look to the left. Please. Please.

ARCHER

(*Slamming the curtain closed*)

Listen, you . . .

IMMANUEL

Do you mind if I slip a bit further under the covers? Only when I lie flat does my spine rest.

ARCHER

Do as you please. You tell Harry that train leaves at eleven and I expect him to be down there packed and ready to leave. I expect . . .

IMMANUEL

I can converse quite well under the covers. I shall direct you from under the covers.

ARCHER

I don't need directions. He's not there. You tell Harry it's track four, track . . .

IMMANUEL

First, do you see the bakery?

ARCHER

(*Slowly returns to the window and draws back the curtain*)
All right. All right.

IMMANUEL

Next to the bakery is a mailbox. You see the mailbox?

ARCHER

I'm not sure. The street is dark.

IMMANUEL

He always wears . . .

ARCHER

I know. I know. A red coat.

IMMANUEL

Always a red coat.

ARCHER

I see the mailbox. After the mailbox is a lamppost. The light is out. Where is he? By the lamppost? Is he by the lamppost?
(*There is no answer from* IMMANUEL. *When* ARCHER

[ 218 ]

*turns around,* IMMANUEL *seems to be asleep. There is a gentle snore or two.* ARCHER *looks down on the bed for a second or two then angrily takes his jacket off the line. As he puts it on preparatory to leaving, he is seized with stomach pains. Once more he walks into the bathroom and cautiously closes the door.* IMMANUEL *immediately throws the covers off and leaps from the bed. He begins vigorously chopping and hacking at the fish*)

IMMANUEL

Sometimes it does not work quite properly. Sometimes the pipes clog and will not flow. Sometimes there is noise and flakes of rust fall. Sometimes the water backs up and thrusts itself through the pores of the weary metal. Sometimes the metal groans and the apparatus shakes. Sometimes the water is stagnant and smells.

ARCHER

It's all right.

IMMANUEL

Do you wish to read?

ARCHER

No.

IMMANUEL

I shall slip your magazine under the door.

ARCHER

Just leave me alone. I'll be out in a second.

IMMANUEL

There is no rush. Do not rush yourself.


ARCHER

I don't want to talk while I'm in the bathroom. All right? (*A few seconds go by*) Where's the toilet paper?


IMMANUEL

There is always a roll in the bathroom.


ARCHER

There's no toilet paper in here.


IMMANUEL

(*Approaching the toilet*)

I will check.


ARCHER

Keep out of here.


IMMANUEL

You must allow the door to open. I will check.


ARCHER

There's no paper in here. I'm not blind. I can see what's here.


IMMANUEL

I will check the cupboard. (*Goes over to the cupboard and looks inside*) We have no toilet paper.


ARCHER

Jesus Christ.

[ 220 ]

IMMANUEL

We have soft table napkins.

ARCHER

All right.

IMMANUEL

*(Reaches into the cupboard and pulls out a single nap-kin. Stands in front of the bathroom door)*
I have it.

ARCHER

*(Opens the door a fraction of an inch.* IMMANUEL *stares in)*
Give me some more of them.

IMMANUEL

That was Harry's responsibility to buy! There is no more! I only buy the food. I am not to blame.

ARCHER

Do you have any Kleenex?

IMMANUEL

There is no Kleenex.
*(He picks up* ARCHER's *copy of the* Saturday Evening Post *and, ripping off the cover, silently passes it under the door.* ARCHER *silently takes it. Some moments pass.* ARCHER *pulls the flush chain. Nothing happens. He violently pulls it a number of times)*

ARCHER

It's not flushing.

[ 221 ]

IMMANUEL

Sometimes there is trouble. I shall come in and help.

ARCHER

Stay out. I'll take care of it myself. (*He climbs on the toilet seat and looks into the water box*) The rod on the float ball is twisted. (*He tries to straighten it by hand*) Damn.

IMMANUEL
(*Shouts*)

It can't be straightened.

ARCHER
(*Still at it*)

Damn it.

IMMANUEL

Aaagh! Some things are worn crooked.

ARCHER
(*With deep anger*)

Anything can be straightened! You could straighten out the whole world if you wanted to. Get me a pair of pliers. The whole world if you had the right attitude. If Columbus didn't think the world was flat he wouldn't have even bothered sailing. They'd still be thinking the earth was going around the sun. You know something is wrong, you get off your butt and you fix it up. You move out. You get on the stick. You put your shoulders to the wheel. You throw up in a plane, you clean it up and keep going. You just don't stand around whining about it. That's how you fix things up. That's how everything gets

straightened. (IMMANUEL *starts limping toward the cupboard*)
Come on. Come on.

(*He returns with the pliers and hands them to* ARCHER)

IMMANUEL

Not everything can be straightened.

ARCHER

Everything can be straightened. Everything. I'll straighten
this. I'll straighten this son of a bitch. Get me some water.
(*While* IMMANUEL *fills up a bucket,* ARCHER *works furiously on
the float ball*) We'll see if it can't be fixed; oh yeah, we'll see
. . . All right . . . Come on with that water. (IMMANUEL
*hands him the bucket.* ARCHER *pours the bucket full of water into
the water box*) All right, we'll see, what can and what can't be
fixed. (*He steps off the toilet seat and pulls the chain. There
is a loud flushing sound*) Oh, God. It's not stopping. It's coming
up. It's coming up. Oh, God!

(ARCHER *comes running out. His feet are soaking wet.
The water flows under the door*)

IMMANUEL

It's Harry's toilet! His! His!

CURTAIN

# Scene Three

*To divide what is thine from what is mine*

PLACE: *Same as Scene Two.*
TIME: *Ten-thirty that night.*
SCENE: *Same as Scene Two.*
ON RISE: IMMANUEL *is huddled under the covers in the bed. There is the sound of the downstairs door slamming. Offstage, we hear* HARRY *shouting.*

### HARRY
*(Offstage)*

Hey, Archie, Archie! (*Pause, then he starts singing and laughing*)

> From this valley they say you are going
> I shall miss your bright eyes and sweet smile
> For they say you are taking the sunshine
> That brightens our pathway awhile.

### HERMAN
*(Offstage, in German)*

Be still, you American bum. American go home! We don't want trash over here.

### HARRY
*(Offstage)*

Sieg Heil! Sieg Heil!

[ 224 ]

HERMAN

(*Offstage, in German*)

I'm going to call the police.

HARRY

(*Offstage, with German accent*)

Achtung, achtung, make ready the gas chamber. Lower the children into the soap vats, knock out the gold teeth.

HERMAN

(*Offstage in English*)

I'm going to call the police.

HERMAN'S WIFE

(*Offstage, in German*)

Don't aggravate yourself, Herman. Come inside.

HARRY

(*On stage*)

Call the Gestapo too, you pot-bellied cretin Nazi bastard. The only reason they didn't get you clowns at Nuremberg was international big business. I'm the one guy who remembers Pearl Harbor. I'm the one guy who doesn't forget. Sieg Heil! Sieg Heil! Right in the fuehrer's face. You want something to remember? I'll give you something to remember. Here it comes. Get set. Here it comes.

(HARRY *runs over to the phonograph and turns it on. It starts with a blare. The song is "The Master Race," a satire on the Germans.* HARRY *goosesteps around the room. Song, on record*)

Ven der fuehrer says, "Ve iss der Master Race,"
Ve heil, ve heil, right in der fuehrer's face.

Not to love der fuehrer iss a great disgrace,
So ve heil, ve heil, right in der fuehrer's face.
Iss ve not der supermen, superduper supermen?
Ya ve iss der supermen, superduper supermen.
Ve bring der Verld to order.
Heil Hitler's vord is order . . .

(*A severe banging begins from* HERMAN's *apartment downstairs.* HARRY *grabs the same stick* IMMANUEL *had used and returns the banging with vicious glee. Runs to the door. Shouts in hall*)

HARRY

I remember Pearl Harbor. Achtung, achtung, make ready the medical experiment.

HERMAN
(*Offstage, in English*)

Chicago gangster!

HERMAN'S WIFE
(*Offstage, in German*)

Come inside, Herman. He is a madman.

HARRY
(*Long Bronx cheer*)

Right in the fuehrer's face. (HERMAN's *door slams shut.* HARRY *shuts his door and leans against it for a moment as if catching his breath. He is breathing hard. He calms down, switches off record in such a way that record just comes to a slow stop. He leans against the door for a few more seconds taking in the situation. A slow smile appears and then in a* "hide and go seek" *voice*) Hey, Archie, Archie, Archie, where is you? (*Harry, pretending to be a combat soldier sneaking up*

[ 226 ]

on the enemy, backs along the wall toward the toilet. He kicks
open the toilet door and machine-guns the area. The game
done, he turns to look at the huddled mass of IMMANUEL *under
the bed covers*) Hey, roach, where's my brother? It's ten-thirty.
Half-hour to train time. Bong! Bong! Hey, cockroach. Come on,
little cockroach. (*Goes over to the bed*) Cockroach? Cockroach? Black Ugly Man is home. Do you know what makes
this night different from all other nights? Do you know why
on this night we have to get our chin whiskers standing taller
than ever tall they stood? It's going back to Ohio night. All the
little lights at *American Farm and Garden* . . . Pow . . . Pow
. . . Pow. My brother waiteth at the station. All things waiteth
on the hour and for me. So let's get those antennae standing
tall, roachcock.

(HARRY *with one sweep pulls the covers halfway off*
IMMANUEL. IMMANUEL *is in a fetal position, his back to*
HARRY)

IMMANUEL
(*Grabbing back the covers*)
What are you doing? (*Throws them back over his head.*
HARRY *starts to pull at the covers.* IMMANUEL *resists*) What are
you doing? What are you doing?

HARRY
(*Imitating him*)
What am I doing? What am I doing?

IMMANUEL
Don't imitate me, Harry. Don't do that.

HARRY
Come on outta there, spider. The web is ripped. The strands

[ 227 ]

playing on the breeze. The hunter is home from the hill, the sailor from the ocean, and the time has come to part, to sunder, to pluck up, to divide what is thine from what is mine.

IMMANUEL

Leave me alone, Harry. If you're going, go.

HARRY

Aw, he was sulking under the covers!

IMMANUEL

I was sleeping, Harry. I was just sleeping.

HARRY

He was sulking because Black Ugly Man was unhibernating himself.

IMMANUEL

I was sleeping.

HARRY

You lying eight-legged son of a bitch. You never sleep. You haven't shut your eyes since DDT. Get the hell out of my bed.
(*Continues pulling at the covers*)

IMMANUEL

A third of the bed is mine, Harry. You'll be late. Your brother wouldn't like that. Leave me alone. The train leaves at eleven. You'll be late.

HARRY

You'd like that. Tell me you'd like that.

[ 228 ]

IMMANUEL

Don't get the covers all mussed up, Harry.

HARRY

Tell me how much you'd like Black Ugly Man to stay, **roach.**
Let me hear it.

IMMANUEL

You know I can't sleep when the covers get all mussed up.

HARRY

Tell me.

IMMANUEL

The sheet's getting all tangled, Harry.

HARRY

Tell me before I pull seven of your legs off.

IMMANUEL

I'm sleeping, Harry. I'm sleeping.

HARRY
(*Stops tugging at the bedding*)

Swear you were sleeping.

IMMANUEL

I don't want to swear, Harry.

HARRY

I want you to swear. Swear!

IMMANUEL

I swear.

HARRY

Swear on something you hold near and dear.

IMMANUEL

I swear on my mother's life.

HARRY

Swear on something sweet and innocent.

IMMANUEL

On the blood of virgins, Harry. My mother is sweet and innocent. On her sainted life.

HARRY

(*While talking he is surreptitiously working to pull
down the clothesline strung across the room*)
You're lying. You're an habitual liar. You lie about everything. The spring, the fall, the winter, flowers, teakettles, bath-
tub rings.

IMMANUEL

Not on my mother's life. I wouldn't swear on my mother's
life and lie, Harry. Not on my . . .

HARRY

You never had a mother.

IMMANUEL

I had a mother, Harry. Her hair should fall out if I'm lying.

HARRY

How about the milk? You lied about that.

IMMANUEL

A mother's life is sacred. Let her tongue hang out if I'm lying.

[ 230 ]

HARRY

You ordered plain and you told me homogenized.

IMMANUEL

Some things are sacred, Harry. It was homogenized.

HARRY

It was plain and you drank off all the butterfat and all the cream with the vitamin A and D and you left the scummy water part for me.

IMMANUEL

In the sacred bowels of Jesus it was a mistake, Harry. I forgot to shake the bottle.

HARRY

You use me all the time. (*Starts imitating him*) Harry, my feet are cold. Harry, scratch my balls. Harry, my ass itches. Harry, buy another fish. And all the time you were skimming off the cream. Every last lousy day.

(*Suddenly* HARRY, *having secured the rope, pulls* IM-MANUEL *widthwise across the bed and begins rolling the mattress up*)

IMMANUEL

What are you doing? My spine. Don't damage the blood vessels into the spine!

HARRY

The thing was you thought you had me. The web here; the plotting board there. You thought this stinking room was it for me. It. Every last lousy day. But I'm bigger than this room! You know I'm bigger than this room.

IMMANUEL

I ordered homogenized. I swear on the Holy Ghost. The Holy Ghost, Harry.

HARRY

(*Begins tying* IMMANUEL *in*)

A thousand times bigger than this room. That's why I'm going back to Ohio. There isn't enough air in this room to last me five minutes. If you took all the air in Europe and put it in this room, it wouldn't be enough.

IMMANUEL

Don't do this to me, Harry. I'm not an animal. Don't tie me up like an animal.

HARRY

(*Finishes tying the rope around the mattress*)

You are an animal! Don't fool yourself, that's all. I got a blue guitar, you know. I see things as they are. You better see things the way they are. Tell me you don't want me to go back to Ohio.

(HARRY *jumps up and down on the mattress*)

IMMANUEL

My spine.

HARRY

Tell me you'd rather have this than Black Ugly Man going back.

IMMANUEL

My spine.

HARRY

Tell me!

#### IMMANUEL

Don't go back, Harry. You're my best comrade, Harry. Till the end of time.

#### HARRY

(*Imitating him*)

Don't go back, Harry. (*Stops the imitation*) Well, it's all up. (*Leaves* IMMANUEL *all trussed up and goes over to the closet. He pulls out a valise and starts throwing odds and ends in it*)

#### IMMANUEL

What are you going to do in America, Harry? Are you going to be a big success in America? Are you going to fight World War II and win Congressional Medals, Harry? Are you going to open up a used-car business and make mountains of money? What are you going back to, Harry?

#### HARRY

It's summer all the time in Ohio. Even when it snows it's summer. In the winter you can hunt unicorns in Ohio. Whole fields of them.

#### IMMANUEL

There are no unicorns in Ohio, Harry. You can't even paint. Why do you think they wouldn't keep you as a student in Florence? Why do you think you only sell your stuff to me? I'm the only one. Isn't it strange? The only one. It seems strange to me. Do you want to go to another art school in America? Lots of damn fine Americans went to Ohio State. Then you can go to another one and another one and another one. You'll never run out of schools. They never let you run out of schools

in America. You can't add. You can't fly. The only thing you
know how to do is vomit in Air Force planes.

HARRY

(*Searching around for something*)

Where's my gym shorts? Where's my tennis balls? Where are
the Florida coconut patties from my sisters? I'll kill you if
you ate them. (*Finds them*) Where's my oxblood shoes? (*Begins searching with intensity*) What did you do with my oxblood shoes?

IMMANUEL

People die in Ohio, Harry. Black things, worms, beetles, flies,
die in Ohio. Things die. Don't forget the lederhosen, Harry.

HARRY

I don't want the lederhosen. I want my oxblood shoes. Nothing dies in Ohio.

IMMANUEL

It isn't Christmas in Ohio. It isn't poetry.

HARRY

Nothing dies in Ohio. Where's my oxblood shoes?

IMMANUEL

I didn't touch them. They're in the closet.

HARRY

I didn't see them. You're lying to me.

IMMANUEL

They're in the closet where you put them.

HARRY

Why can't I see them then? Why can't I find them if they're in the closet? I'm not going to be cheated out of my shoes.

IMMANUEL

They're in the closet, Harry. What's the matter with you?

HARRY

Why can't I find them then. I can't find them. They're not here.

IMMANUEL

They are, Harry.

HARRY

(*Starts jumping up and down on the mattress*)
They're not here. I won't go without them.

IMMANUEL

My spine. My bones.

HARRY

Don't give me that spine shit. What did you do with what's mine?

IMMANUEL

Remember when I bought the lederhosen for you, Harry? The sparrows had come back to Munich and they were standing in the snow puddles like thin sticks. You said everybody was wearing lederhosen and you wanted a pair and I took the check my father sent me and I spent it all for you.

HARRY

You didn't touch my stuff all day today?

IMMANUEL

I don't want to play the games, Harry.

HARRY

You didn't touch my stuff all day today?

IMMANUEL

(*After a pause. Suddenly with loud sincerity*)
I swear on the Virgin's womb. The fruit of the womb. On the holy fingers of the Magi, Harry.

HARRY

You didn't touch my two thirds of the dresser? You didn't stick your hands in my two thirds of the dresser and put on my stuff and show my stuff off to your friends?

IMMANUEL

My mother's breasts should rot if I touched anything of yours.

HARRY

I can tell if you touched my drawers. You know what? Should I tell you how I always know when you're fondling my stuff? Should I tell you? (*Turns the mattress around so that IM-MANUEL faces the dresser. HARRY goes over to the dresser*) You think I put paper matches in the corner and the matches fall to the floor when the drawer's opened. So all you had to do was replace the matches and I wouldn't know. Well, it wasn't the matches. The matches are a decoy. That's how you get fooled. A decoy. It was the talcum powder. All along the edges I put talcum powder and when anything is touched the talcum powder falls to the floor. Puddles of talcum. You thought it was the paper matches, didn't you?
(*Pulls the drawer. Talcum falls*)

IMMANUEL

I never touched your dresser!

HARRY

So you opened the drawer, slowly, slowly, and then carefully
put back the match. But you overlooked one detail. One small
detail.

IMMANUEL

I can't feel my legs, Harry. My rib cage is bending.

HARRY

The secret's in the talcum powder. I put the talcum powder
in the shoes and when you wore them there were footprints. In
the crotch of the pants, too. Last week the corduroy pants.
(*Runs to closet, pulls out the corduroy pants and shoves them
in front of* IMMANUEL) You see that? (*Turns them upside down
and the talcum falls out*) You don't do a damn thing I don't
know about.
      (*Crawls up on top of the mattress and reaching over into
      the night table grabs handfuls of talcum and begins throw-
      ing them inside the mattress*)

IMMANUEL

Don't treat me like this. I can't breathe.

HARRY

You can breathe.

IMMANUEL

I can't breathe.

HARRY

      (*Jumping up and down on mattress*)
You can breathe. You throw the covers over your head. You

breathe that, don't you? You breathe stale air, old air, used air. The air people forget about: in closets, in corners, old tires. Last week's air. Last year's air. When did you change the air in this room? Did you change it last week when I told you to?

IMMANUEL

I did. By Christ's holy bladder I did.

HARRY

The hell you did.

IMMANUEL

(*Excited by being able to prove the air was changed*)
We had bluefish a week ago. There's no bluefish smell in the room. Smell, smell.

HARRY

When we were in Rome . . . (*Imitates* IMMANUEL'S *voice*) "Harry, let's stay down in the catacombs just another hour. Let me suck up the air around the crypts just another minute."

IMMANUEL

I'm telling the truth by the warm milk in Mary's bosom. Just smell. One smell.

HARRY

All right, I'm going to do that. I'm going to do that. (*Stops and smells*) It's that same goddam fish smell.

IMMANUEL

It's not, Harry. This is codfish. I bought a codfish. The first Friday of every month it's a sardine fish, then a pickerel fish, then a bluefish, then a codfish.

[ 238 ]

HARRY

(*Reaches over and picks up the black glove that is lying on the night table*)

You wore the rubber glove?

IMMANUEL

You know what we'll do. We'll go skiing at Garmisch. You always wanted to do that, Harry. Just us. Juju and Michael won't know. We can spend all winter huddling and cuddling and drinking rum. We'll buy ski outfits as soon as my check comes. You always wanted a white ski outfit.

HARRY

But you wore the glove for Archer?

IMMANUEL

He was confused. I spoke of illnesses and touched him. I touched his arm and the flesh below shrank. I spoke of skin conditions and infirmities. I hinted at certain handicaps, at foul odors that emanate from the mouth, at smells that rise between the toes.

HARRY

And then the suggestions of greasy skin and scales on the thighs? You didn't forget about that and the soaps and salts?

IMMANUEL

I thrust my leg through the robe. He was confused. He rose slightly in the chair, fell back, gazed away.

HARRY

He does that. When I used to ask him for things or try to tell him things he would look up to the ceiling.

IMMANUEL

I mentioned the blood vessels. Infirmities. The lack of hair.

HARRY

Archer is covered with hair. The whole family is hairy.

IMMANUEL

I suggested vague disorders that could not be cleansed.

HARRY

They bathe twice a day. God, they hate dirt.

IMMANUEL

Vague illnesses involving worms and acnes.

HARRY

And the ones with Latin names? You didn't forget the ones with Latin names?

IMMANUEL

I remembered them all. He was weakening. I twisted my leg and perfumed it. I spoke of colds and snows and exquisite suffering. Encasements in ice and the tortures of tearing ligaments. I called him to my side.

HARRY

That was when he resisted.

IMMANUEL

I slid his hand upon my shoulder. "But my throat is warm. Feel my throat. Do my shoulders seem hot or cold? The left is warmer than the right. My heart is cold. Feel my back. The hump is hot. Feel my hump."

[ 240 ]

HARRY

You did the hump? That's when you found out about his iron will. Right? Right? That was the moment when you had to stop. That iron will.

IMMANUEL

But it was too late, Harry. He felt less, that he was reduced. I could see it in his eyes.

HARRY

Had you done the beads?

IMMANUEL

The crucifix, too, and the holy water and then the nail relics. I made him touch the nails.

HARRY

But he wasn't overcome. He has perfect control. He never loses control!

IMMANUEL

He moved to the window, but it wasn't the same man. He was reduced, confused, less than he was. "You will not look at the convent." "No." "You must not look at the convent." "I won't look at the convent." "Don't look at the convent." I had my rubber glove on, my twisted spine, my hump and my limp. He didn't want to sit on the bed, but he sat. He didn't want to stroke me, but he did. The powder had risen about him; it clung to his coat; he couldn't shake himself free; the church bells rang and he was less and less and then he couldn't find the balloon man, but he kept looking, and I directed him. I was in command. "Can you see the bakery? Can you see the mailbox?" He was growing weaker, a bull weakened by a dozen pics. I didn't relent. I moved further below the covers. I was conquering, his will was collapsing. I ran him through, Harry. I ran the bull through. I could feel the bleeding in my mouth, I . . .

HARRY

Oh Goddam you! God *damn* you!
(*He begins pulling the mattress off the bed with* IM-MANUEL *inside.* HARRY *is in a real panic*)

IMMANUEL

You are pleased! You are. I did it for you.

HARRY

You did it for yourself.

IMMANUEL

You wanted it. You wanted me to do it. You couldn't do it.
(*He screams out like a madman while* HARRY *drags him across the floor*)

HARRY

I didn't want it.

IMMANUEL

You wanted it.

HARRY

Never! I never wanted it. Never. Not once. Not one time. Not to my brother.

IMMANUEL

Always. Everything you did, you wanted it. I did it for you. You knew he was coming. You got out. You left him for me.

HERMAN

(*At that moment* HERMAN *shouts up the stairway, off-stage, and his* WIFE *starts banging on the ceiling*)
You crazy maniacs. I'm going to have you locked up in an insane asylum. Do you hear! Stop that noise!

HARRY

(*Jumping up and down on the floor.* HERMAN'S WIFE *answers by banging up.* HARRY *runs over to the door and opens it*)
Where were you when they were turning people into soap? When they were making lampshades? What were you doing then? What about the noise then? Why didn't you hear the noise then when they needed you? Who needs you now?

HERMAN
(*Offstage*)
I'm going to call the police.

HARRY

Call the police. (*Looks around the apartment for something to throw*) I'll give you something to call the police for. Let them throw me in a concentration camp. I'm not afraid of your lousy concentration camps.
(*Grabs a flowerpot. Runs out into the hall*)

HERMAN
(*Offstage*)
You madman.

HARRY

You son of a bitch.
(*Throws the flowerpot. It evidently strikes* HERMAN, *who is coming up the stairs. We hear him fall down the stairs*)

[ 243 ]

HERMAN'S WIFE

(*Offstage in German*)

My God. My God. You've killed him!

HARRY

You open your mouth. I got one for you, lampshade-maker.
Heil Hitler.

(*Runs back, grabs another flowerpot*)

IMMANUEL

(*Screaming out*)

Harry! Harry!

(HARRY *runs to stairwell. Throws flowerpot. This one
misses. We hear it break*)

HERMAN'S WIFE

(*Runs down the stairs, screaming in German*)

He's killed my husband. Help! Police!

HARRY

You think it's enough if you keep the railroad stations clean?
It's not enough. You gotta keep clean in the heart. In the heart.
You Nazi bitch. Call the storm troopers. Nazi bitch! You don't
fool me. (*Runs over to the window. Flings it open. Shouts out*)
You Nazi bitch! (*Starts wandering around the room*) You
crazy. You crazy. You crazy.

IMMANUEL

Harry, you must run from here. She's going to call the police.
You don't know our police, Harry.

HARRY

What do I care about your lousy police. Where are my ox-
bull shoes? My ox-bull shoes!

[ 244 ]

IMMANUEL

They'll take you away. Get out of here. Go back to the Dolly
Bar. I'll meet you. What do we care about the rest of the world?

HARRY

What are you talking about? I'm meeting my brother at the
bahnhof at eleven. I want a drink of water.

IMMANUEL

There isn't time.
   (*He struggles to free himself but he cannot.* HARRY *goes
over to the refrigerator and pours out some of the "holy"
water. He drinks it. Watches almost with detachment* IM-
MANUEL's *struggles with the mattress*)

HARRY

   (*Tapping the empty glass against his teeth*)
You'll never get out. Once you're in, you're in. It's mathe-
matics. It's figured on computers. Columns add up. Add up one
side, add up another side. So much for this side. So much for
that side.

IMMANUEL

Get out of here, Harry. Please. Please.

HARRY

   (*Refills the glass and walks over*)
There's always been something I've wanted to see. You know
what that is?

IMMANUEL

There isn't time.

HARRY

(*Sits down beside* IMMANUEL)

I've always wanted to know if a clown is a clown always —
if you are a clown or not a clown.

IMMANUEL

I'm not a clown, Harry. (HARRY *sticks his hand in the mattress and begins pulling* IMMANUEL's *head out*) Leave me alone,
Harry.

HARRY

I'm gonna pull your head out.

IMMANUEL

You're hurting me. I'm hurt, Harry.

(HARRY *finally succeeds in pulling* IMMANUEL's *head out.
He pushes the glass filled with water in front of* IM-
MANUEL's *mouth*)

HARRY

You gotta get the glass in your teeth. I want you to pick up
the glass and drink the water.

IMMANUEL

I can't get my arms out.

HARRY

You gotta drink it without your arms.

IMMANUEL

I can't.

HARRY

This is confidential. Entre nous, you know what I mean?

IMMANUEL

There isn't time.

HARRY

Don't worry about time. You have nothing to do with time. This is about the circus that came to Columbus when I was in the Cub Scouts.

IMMANUEL

I don't want to hear about circuses, Harry. I want to go skiing at Garmisch.

HARRY

Archer said that the clowns were clowns even when they weren't wearing clown suits. How about that? Isn't that an amazing thing to hear? What do you think about it? Isn't it amazing?

IMMANUEL

It's stupid, Harry.

HARRY

But it implies things. You see that? You see how it implies things? Once you're in, you're in. What do you think?

IMMANUEL

I don't know.

HARRY

Neither did I, then. But after the circus, Archer took me downstairs below the arena to see Moko. Moko was a failure clown. The kind that everything goes wrong for. He just wants to get out of the arena. But they won't let him. That's essential.

[ 247 ]

They won't let him go. He tries to climb the wall, but he keeps falling back, so they try to shoot him out of a cannon, but the cannon won't fire. It blows up in his face. He runs to the phony doors they keep shoving in front of him, but the doors won't open. They drag him over to a spinning ball, but he can't stay on. He runs up to the other clowns for help, but they throw water on him. He can't win. The other clowns steal his shoes; they beat him up. They lie to him. They kick him in the behind. And all this time he's saying, "God, let me escape; God, let me escape."

IMMANUEL

This has nothing to do with me, Harry. I don't want to listen.

HARRY

I'm shouting, "Let him go. What do you want from him?" But my sisters and Archer are laughing.

IMMANUEL

Let me out, Harry. Please. Please.

HARRY

So Archer takes me under the arena and there's Moko sitting in front of his dressing table. An old, old man bent over. Archer doesn't knock. He doesn't even knock! Most of the paint is off. Long silver lines of tears running down Moko's face. God! I remember that. How weird. He looks up into the mirror and stares at us and then he turns around with the saddest expression I ever saw. I wanted to cry, but Archer starts laughing and laughing. And Moko got sadder and sadder. Archer couldn't stop laughing. He kept trying to turn away and Moko wouldn't let him. Archer ran all over the arena and Moko kept chasing him and chasing him around and around making him look, sticking his face in front of him. When I cried, Archer laughed, it was always that way, but now Archer had to hold his ribs. The clown wanted to kill him.

IMMANUEL

I want to get out of here, Harry. I don't want to be tied up.

HARRY

It's not a matter of what you want! It's a matter of what you get. Drink!

IMMANUEL

I'm not a clown.

HARRY

Try. You never know till you try.

IMMANUEL

I don't want to try. I'm not a clown. I'm a human being, Harry.

(IMMANUEL *looks up at him, pleadingly.* HARRY *stares mutely at him.* IMMANUEL *takes the glass in his teeth and, painfully raising his head, drinks. The glass falls out of his mouth and the water spills to the floor.* HARRY *wearily gets up*)

HARRY

You see how you dropped it? You couldn't do it. You're a clown after all. That's the way it is with clowns. They think they can make it till every cannon in the world blows up in their face, till every ball slips out under their feet. You start out life thinking you can do it. Nobody has got you down for pantaloons and colored hair because you're just starting out. You haven't vomited in the plane yet. You think, boy, I'm go-

ing to sail! Boy, I'm going to get out of that cannon with a flying roar! Boy, I'm going to get in that sky and really move!
Your brother is sailing in the blue, your sisters are sailing in the
blue, the whole God-clean world is sailing in the blue, and
you're fading out. You're dimming. You've got a green head.
You got purple eyes. Whoever is in, you're out. You're growing
radishes in swamps, you're doing it all wrong, nothing's coming
up. Maybe they won't notice you're dimming. You never make
it. In or out. In or out. Right from the beginning. (*Sound of a
police car.* HARRY *picks up the statue of the stone-blind kid and
puts it near his valise*) Out on the ocean by tomorrow. The
wind blowing clean. Skimming. Cutting the water like a knife.
America. America.

IMMANUEL

Oh, Harry.

HARRY

You keep quiet. I wanna see those shoes produced. That's
what I want from you.

(*Sound of people running up the stairs*)

HERMAN'S WIFE
(*Offstage, in German*)

This way. This way. He dropped a flowerpot on my husband's head. He is a madman.

HARRY
(*Closes his valise and touches the statue*)

I'm gonna give him eyes to see with. Big granite eyes.

POLICEMAN
(*Offstage, in German*)

This is the police. Open up.

[ 250 ]

HARRY

Anne Frank doesn't live here. You wanna find Anne Frank?
She's dead. Gone.

(HARRY *runs over to the record player and starts a new*
*record. It is "The Emperor's Waltz"*)

POLICEMAN
(*Offstage, in German*)

Open up.

HARRY

She's gone away. Heil Hitler. This is the fuehrer speaking.
Tomorrow we will put on the clown moustaches and make with
the goosestepping.

POLICEMAN
(*Offstage, in English this time*)

If you do not open up, I will force the door.

HARRY

Go ahead. I'm an American. I'm sure the American ambassa-
dor will be interested in the revival of Nazi fascism.

(*The door is forced*)

HERMAN'S WIFE
(*Standing back a bit. In German*)

That's him.

HARRY

I wish to prefer charges against this woman.

HERMAN'S WIFE

You madman. You want to kill. That's what you want.

HARRY
(*In German*)

She is a war criminal.

POLICEMAN
(*In English*)
We will talk this over at the police station, sir.

HARRY

Talk it over here. I've an eleven o'clock appointment. (*The policeman grabs* HARRY. HARRY *resists and is forced down the stairwell. He screams out*) Hey, wait a minute. Wait a minute, you fascist. Can't you wait just a minute? Just that minute. I'm an American. Just that minute. I'm an American. I am an American. (*As soon as they have left the room,* IMMANUEL *begins violently struggling to free himself. He rolls about the floor with maniacal determination and desperation. The bells of the convent are tolling. Far down the stairwell* HARRY *calls out*) Archer! Archer!
(IMMANUEL *answers in a voice full of rage*)

IMMANUEL

Me, Harry. What about me? Me!
(*The music on the record player, "The Emperor's Waltz," has grown very loud. It fills the entire room with the glorious sounds of another era. The spotlight focussed on* IM-MANUEL's *enraged face suddenly blacks out, leaving the stage in darkness and a cacophony of suddenly stopped sound*)

CURTAIN